D0021495

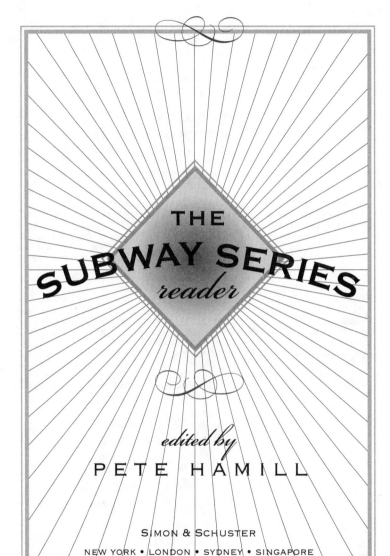

THE
SUBWAY SERIES
reader

edited by

PETE HAMILL

SIMON & SCHUSTER

NEW YORK • LONDON • SYDNEY • SINGAPORE

SIMON & SCHUSTER
Rockefeller Center
1230 Avenue of the Americas
New York, New York 10020

CONTENTS

INTRODUCTION

PETE HAMILL

- I -

ONCE UPON A TIME there was a magical republic whose young citizens believed that anything in life was possible. All they had to do was work hard and they could grow up to become movie stars or master detectives. Children of factory workers could become doctors or lawyers or president of the United States. If they worked very hard, and had some luck, they could be left fielders for the Dodgers. Or shortstops for the Giants. Or pitchers for the Yankees. Or third basemen for all three teams. Work was the key, because in that republic work was essential to magic.

The republic was situated on islands, separated by rivers and a great harbor, and its streets were often luminous with a marine light. The climate was drastic: winters of deep snows and black ice, summers of thick smothering heat. But one month of the year was filled with a special dazzle. Nights in that month were cool but not bitter cold. Breezes tossed the hair of women, and men walked the avenues without overcoats. The month was called October. The island republic was called New York.

The snows and heat and the month of October were, of course, common to each of the five sections that made up the city: Manhattan, Brooklyn and the Bronx, Queens and Staten Island. They were connected by bridges, ferries, and an underground railroad system that the inhabitants called the subway. Since there were few automobiles in the time of which I speak (citizens could not afford them), millions used the subway. It was as essential to their lives as breathing. They took the subway when they went to work in the glittering towers of Manhattan, or to shop in the great bazaars, to attend schools, or to sample the bawdy entertainments of a souk called Times Square. On the subway, there were usually only two destinations: a place of endless possibility or a place called home.

Home was located in one of the urban hamlets that we called neighborhoods. In essence, these resembled every other hamlet in America, possessing their own local dialects and myths, fools and wastrels and big shots, their few wise men and their busy gossips. In New York, ethnicity and class also played a role. There were Irish neighborhoods and Italian neighborhoods, Jewish neighborhoods and African American neighborhoods. There were well-defended hamlets for the rich and dead zones for the poor. But all had a common denominator in the form of a secular religion. That religion was called baseball.

- II -

I realize looking back now at my magical republic that it probably never existed. No city could have been as big and proud and wonderful as New York was after World War Two. No young Americans ever could have been as optimistically innocent as we were from 1946 to 1957. In the worst years of twentieth-century New York (roughly 1975 to 1995), when the city was being mauled each day by decay, poverty, crack cocaine, and ferocious violence, I'd think back to that time and place. Then I would ache for its simplicities, decencies, and certainties. The defining metaphor for such lost innocence was baseball.

Most of the time I succeeded in erasing that part of my own past. But then suddenly one evening in the bad times, and usually in October, I'd see a television clip of the Brooklyn Dodgers. Black and white and grainy. Just as suddenly, and only for a few jagged seconds, my eyes would well with tears—absurdly, and without thought. I'd try to explain to my wife or my daughters, but my voice would crack and I'd stop. In my mind I was seeing men named Snider and Hodges and Furillo when they were young and I was even younger. Podres was pitching. Campanella was at the bat with the bases loaded. I was lost again in a vast crowd in the fall of the year, everyone joined, everyone roaring, and there was Robinson, rounding third, headed for home.

The moment would pass. The present would replace the past. And at night I'd accuse myself of mindless sentimentality. You were just a kid then, I'd say during such late-night reveries. You were full of adolescent illusions. You think you're mourning for a city, but you are really mourning for your own vanished youth. This is maudlin rubbish. Give it up.

But even in such quarrels with myself, lying in the dark, fighting for sleep, a smaller, more tentative voice would emerge, tempered by doubt and experience. This emotional longing is *not* sentimentality, that voice insisted. The city you remember was real. You lived in it. You were there. The magical sense of possibility was real. The people were real. Their pride in work and struggle was real. And one thing was absolutely real: you lived in a neighborhood where almost everybody worshipped at the church of baseball.

In the autumn of the year 2000, images of vanished glories and lost idylls came flooding back and refused to go away in a few seconds. The Yankees overcame a disastrous September to beat the Seattle Mariners for the American League pennant. The wild-card New York Mets conquered the St. Louis Cardinals to become champions of the National League. For the first time since 1956, two New York teams would play each other in a World Series. A *Subway Series*? After forty-four years? That itself was an astonishment. I was one of millions who thought we'd never see such an event again.

In a way, the record of New York baseball from 1947 to 1956 is proof of the validity of memory. The facts are simple: during those ten seasons, there were seven Subway Series. That is to say, in seven out of ten years *two* New York teams played for the world championship of baseball. The Yankees were in every one of them, the Dodgers in six, and the New York Giants in one (1951, the year Bobby Thomson hit the home run in a playoff game to beat the Dodgers). Of the seven Subway Series, the Yankees won six, finally losing to the Dodgers in 1955 but beating them again in the following October. That was the last Subway Series. There were only eight teams in each league, and none west of the Mississippi, but such domination of a sport by one city had never been seen before and has never been equaled since. You could look it up.

But simply stating the baseball facts is not enough to explain the tangled emotions that still roil the hearts of so many people who were young in those years. Many of the pieces in this book are about the present, as they should be: about *these* Yankees and *these* Mets. And we who are cursed with longer memories are absolutely realistic about the present. We know that Derek Jeter is a better shortstop (with glove and bat) than anyone who played the position in our youth. We know that Mariano Rivera is better than any relief pitcher we saw then. We also know what we didn't know when we were young: that baseball is just a part of the entertainment industry. Its goal is to make money for owners, not to provide some secular form of spiritual union. It's certainly not a religion, peopled by saints. Many old Dodgers and Giants are dead and the survivors are even older than we are. Ebbets Field and the Polo Grounds will not rise magically some foggy morning from the congested lots of Flatbush or Harlem. What's gone is gone.

And yet . . . and yet, against all reason, in spite of the cold facts, those emotions remain. They are no longer raw; most of the psychic wounds have long since healed, covered now with scar tissue. But the old Dodger and Giant fans who gave a provisional, ironic loyalty to the Mets after they became the city's National League expansion team in 1962 are cynical about the game in a very personal way. They despise the owners. They think too many present-day ballplayers are overpaid, surly itinerants with no regard for the fans or the towns in which they work. They might root, in a distracted hometown way, for one of the New York teams, but they'll never again allow a baseball team to break their hearts. Irony is their armor. Indifference is their general strategy.

And yet . . . the imminence of a Subway Series touched all of them in some way. Long-buried emotions were suddenly, unexpectedly released. The feelings were not simply about the abilities of players and the cohesiveness of teams, about winning and losing, about champagne showers in locker rooms or championship flags flapping in a summer wind. The emotions were not about bragging rights, or loud-mouthed triumphalism in saloons. The emotions of the old New Yorkers were really about time. Their time. That time.

- III -

When World War Two ended in August 1945, the hamlets of New York were no different from all the other hamlets in America. I was ten years old that summer, and remember the explosion of exuberant noise on the afternoon of V-J day: people beating pots in top-floor windows, music and dancing in the streets, the doors of saloons wide open and the proprietors rolling kegs of free beer out onto the sidewalk. There was a city-wide block party that day, on our block, on every block in every borough. Women laughed and danced; their men were coming home. Men cried; their sons or brothers were coming home too.

In the following spring, the veterans were back. Or most of them. In our hamlet, as in every American hamlet, a painted memorial went up on a wall, adorned with American flags, listing the names of those who would not come back. Most were men who would be twenty-one forever.

We boys would watch the surviving veterans out on the empty streets on Saturday mornings. They played (with the younger men) a game we called stickball, using a broom handle for a bat and a pink rubber ball called a Spaldeen. The field was the street itself, with bases chalked on macadam. The outfield lay beyond an avenue, and the right-field stands were the roof of the factory where my father worked. In memory, those games were filled with a muscular gladness that I've seldom seen in any other time or place. The veterans were, of course, our heroes. "Do you see that man at bat?" someone would murmur, with respect and awe. "He was in the Battle of the Bulge." Or Okinawa. Or Anzio. And we were thrilled. That man at bat had been in all those places whose names we knew from the war maps in the *Daily News*. He'd helped kick the crap out of Hitler or Tojo. And here he was, playing ball on a street in our hamlet. Sipping beer from a cardboard container between innings. Smoking Camels. Saying not a word about the war. Who cared if he grounded out?

Hearing the phrase *Subway Series*, I saw the faces of those men scribbled through my mind. I know now that they must have carried the memory of Saturday-morning stickball through all the bad places of Europe and the South Pacific. Those games I watched were proof of their survival. That hot Saturday morning game was the reward for coming through a long hard time. Stickball, and one other thing.

The other thing seemed to always happen on Sundays. In late morning, after mass, you would see the vets gather outside the saloons of our American hamlet, bars called Rattigan's and Fitzgerald's and Diamond's. The stickball players were there, and so were the men who didn't play ball, the men who had lost an arm or a leg far from home. They all smoked Camels and Chesterfields and Lucky Strikes, and in the spring they wore fedoras. If you drifted close to them and listened, they were talking about women and prizefighters and jobs. Mostly jobs. They made jokes we boys didn't understand, and laughed most of the time. Then, around noon, they would all go off together, and the place to which they were going was Ebbets Field.

They didn't use the subway, since the branch of the subway system that came to our hamlet didn't stop anywhere near Ebbets Field. There was no direct trolley car, either, so most of the time they walked. Nobody in that time and place owned a car. So they left early and walked together across Prospect Park, merging with tribes from other Brooklyn hamlets who were following different paths to the same holy place. Sometimes we kids tagged along. We couldn't afford to pay our own way into the ballpark, but there were free tickets for certain games from the Police Athletic League, and sometimes the veterans had extras and other men gave away unused ducats (pronounced "duckits") at the gates. My father took me to my first game, as did fathers from all American hamlets. That first trip to Ebbets Field was a genuine rite of passage, a small entry into the adult world previously glimpsed only in newspapers or heard about on the radio (for there was no television then). But my friends and I sensed from the beginning that a seat in the bleachers was a complicated matter. We could sit among men and heroes. But we were also adhering to a faith. When we cheered the Dodgers along with many thousands of others, we were accepting an identity card. It was understood that such an acceptance was for life.

There were moments in those first games when I realized how much they meant to those who had made it home from the war. After the start of the games, my friends and I would sometimes wander from the cheap seats down into the lower stands. We hoped to find empty seats behind third base or back of home plate, where we could see the faces of the players. Most of the time we were chased by ushers (all large beefy men who looked like off-duty homicide cops). But occasionally we'd see a man sitting alone, looking down at the sweet green grass amidst the clamor and the roar, tears coursing down his cheeks.

For such men, a ball game at Ebbets Field must have represented final proof that all the wars were over. There would be no corpses at the end of this contest, no boys screaming for medics, no wrecked young men crying the names of women they loved. They would hear no artillery. They would not tremble under mortar attacks, their faces smeared with the mud of Italy or Guadalcanal. Here the loudest sound was a combination of the crack of a bat and the roar from the stands. The rest was hot dogs and beer.

The joyous emotions swirling through the park came from people who had survived the hardest years of the American twentieth century. All of them, veterans and civilians, men and women, had come through a fifteen-year period of deprivation and loss. It had started in 1930, when the Depression began to lay waste to every hamlet in America, closing factories, turning farms into wastelands, wrecking families, stunting Americans in ways that left upon all of them what the historian Caroline Bird called an invisible scar. The young men who fought the war were the tough children of the Depression. The older men and women had endured its soul-grinding, humiliating power. Proud men who worked with their hands and their backs accepted the shame of "relief" to put bowls of barley soup on their family tables. Now the war was over, and the Depression was a memory. Women who had wept too often in the dark now sat beside those proud humbled men in a great glad place. Those women too were toughened by the Depression; like Scarlett O'Hara, they must have vowed that they'd never be hungry again.

Each Brooklyn neighborhood, in short, was like every other American hamlet of that specific time. Men who had learned from war the indispensable value of the team and the unit—its mimicking of the family—now traveled together to watch a team sport. That meant baseball. Professional football still had no place in the American imagination (and most veterans had seen enough of helmets and violence to last a lifetime). Hockey was played by Canadians. The National Basketball Association was not yet formed. Baseball might not be the American pastime, but in those years it was certainly the American game. Naturally the New York fans rooted for the home team. Brooklyn was home to the Dodger fans, Manhattan to the Giant fans, the Bronx (and its annex, Westchester) to many of the Yankee fans. If they'd lived in a hamlet in St. Louis, they'd have rooted for the Cardinals.

And so baseball and home were impossible to separate in those years, because the idea of home contained the innocent pleasures of baseball. We might hate the Yankees, we might despise certain ballplayers on other teams, but in the end, they were not Nazis.

- IV -

This Subway Series provoked many comparisons to the New York past, but the clearest difference in the game itself was visible on the field. African Americans had been playing big league ball since the time of Jackie Robinson in 1947. Now the sport was played by many Latin Americans and by Asians, and an estimated 40 percent of big league ballplayers were foreign-born. In the year 2000, professional baseball looked more than ever like the country in which it was played for the most money before the largest crowds.

But the people in the stands were different too. In the year 2000, the United States was in the midst of the largest immigration wave in a century. Many of these new arrivals were absorbed by New York, the port through which most of the earlier European immigrants had passed on their way to enriching America. To be sure, millions of new immigrants have gone to Los Angeles and Chicago and every other large American city, and many are scattered through rural places, the vast majority doing work that native-born Americans will no longer do. But New York is a city of immigrants, and of their children and grandchildren, and for all its harsh reputation remains a welcoming and tolerant metropolis. The immigrants I meet in New York display their newfound local citizenship by initially bitching and moaning and then saying they would not live anywhere else. For them, everything seems possible, if not for themselves, then for their children. Here, they tell you, all you must do is work.

Many seem to have understood the same lessons learned by my own immigrant father: baseball is the swiftest route to becoming an American. Billy Hamill of Belfast, Northern Ireland, surely learned more about being an American from reading Dick Young in the New York *Daily News* than he could have gotten from *The Federalist Papers*. But for the new arrivals, as for my father, it is sometimes difficult to crack the

American codes. When I was editing the *Daily News*, one Chinese immigrant reader (male) called, in an embarrassed way, to ask us to run a very simple feature: how to read a box score.

Some of today's foreign-born baseball fans come out to see their own kind. The Japanese of Westchester turned out by the thousands to see Hideo Nomo in his first marvelous season; Koreans cheer for Chan Ho Park; Dominicans have their own huge favorites from a country whose leading export seems to be shortstops. But many follow the game without regard to the ethnicity of the players. They identify with one quality more than all others: the attempt at excellence. They don't care about the past, my past, the New York past. Only the present and the future matter: the New York present, the American future. They work too hard to find much time to go to ballparks, but you can see them in bars and bodegas studying televised games as if they were some live-action version of the Rosetta stone.

And thus in the streets of New York, as the pennant races tightened in September, and then vaulted into playoffs and finally to the certainty of a Subway Series, I began noticing a phenomenon I'd never before witnessed: Pakistanis and Koreans and Russians wearing Yankee or Met caps, along with Mexicans and Dominicans and Chinese. On the subways, I'd hear them speaking their own languages, carried with them from their versions of the Old Country, but the sentences were sprinkled with common nouns: Piazza and Agbayani, Franco and Leiter, Torre and Valentine, Williams and O'Neill. This choosing of sides, this identification with an American sport in an American city, was not surprising, but it was so old it was new. And it was exhilarating. Those new immigrants wore their Met and Yankee caps—and sometimes team jackets too—as if they were naturalization papers. Which, in a very important way, they were.

This present would swiftly become part of their own American past. Even the Met fans will remember the time as a happy one, shared with their American children, an October when the greatest of all cities—their magical city—stopped still to focus on baseball. Or so it would seem, up there, in the future.

- V -

When I was asked by the *New York Post* to cover this Subway Series, I accepted without a moment's pause. As a boy, I never saw a World Series game. The prices were too high. Nobody gave away tickets. A World Series seat was for Frank Sinatra or Toots Shor, for President Eisenhower or the mayor of New York. So I absolutely had to go to this one, to complete some unfinished circle. I had a glorious time.

The five games, as all could see, were splendid examples of classic baseball. Every game was contested. Three were settled by a one-run margin. Nobody on the field was humiliated. Even after Roger Clemens hurled his bat at Mike Piazza in the second game, there was a remarkable absence of vehemence among the fans. To be sure, the games were bloated by the demands of the television ad salesmen. Not an inning was played in daylight, where the fine hard sun of October might have added a sense of beauty unique to the time and place. The food peddled in the ballparks was overpriced and wretched. But the baseball was marvelous.

The pieces in this book are proof that baseball is never a simple matter. Statistics are central to the games and their histories, but statistics are not all. Baseball is a drama played without a script. The players have plans and scouting reports and intuitions and experience; they also know that in all the decades of baseball, not a single game has ever been exactly like any other game. If you're a fan, you arrive at the ballpark with your own scenarios in your head, full of hope and the temptations of prophecy. Sometimes you are crushed. Sometimes you are disappointed. Often you are elated. But you are always surprised.

And for a game so obsessed with stats, much reaction is subjective. As this book demonstrates, writers can look at the same games and see them in different ways. So can the fans. Yankee fans saw different games than Met fans, and the differences are sometimes surprising. In his first at-bat at Yankee Stadium, Mike Piazza was booed by Yankee fans, presumably for having the effrontery to survive a Roger Clemens beanball thrown in July. But no chorus of Met fans booed Derek Jeter, who was beating their team with glove and bat. I don't mean that the reactions were universal or even consistent; the crowds, after all, change every night too. But fans, like writers, bring their own personal histories to games and see them in their own special ways. Many of us wished on certain evenings, even in the press box, that we could leave behind the traditions of our craft and cheer or boo with all the others.

Out in the rest of the country, where the World Series ratings were the lowest in history, many citizens showed their irrational hatred for New York by refusing to watch the games at all. Some of this contempt was surely driven by old-fashioned parochialism. Some must have come from the enduring caricature of a swaggering, arrogant, rude New York, an image that has little to do anymore with New York's reality. Part of it also was based on a belief that the New York teams had bought their Subway Series. There was a bit of truth in this, but not much: yes, the Yankees have the highest payroll in the game and the Mets are third. But the Los Angeles Dodgers were second in payroll and never even made the playoffs. The Oakland Athletics were twenty-third in payroll and the St. Louis Cardinals were eleventh. Both came very close to going to the World Series. I've traveled all over the United States and lived in some of its cities, and I still don't fully understand the vehemence about New York and the people who live in its hamlets. But this I do know: those who hate New York cheated themselves of some splendid baseball.

Those games, the players, and the city itself are examined in this book from many perspectives, like the facets in a cubist painting. My own highlight film is a simple one. As an old National League fan, I was rooting for the Mets. But I cherish Paul O'Neill's ten-pitch at-bat in Game 1. It's an old-guy thing: in the last month of the season, O'Neill looked his age, which was thirty-seven. His body was breaking down. His hip was injured. His swing was flawed by his adjustment to pain. But in the ninth inning of Game 1 he gritted his way through an at-bat that changed the game. He drew a walk, and would score the tying run. The Yankees went on to win in the twelfth inning of a four-hour-and-fifty-one-minute baseball game, the longest in Series history.

I loved the sight of Benny Agbayani in Game 3, doubling off El Duque to score Todd Zeile and break a tie. In the Met dugout before the games began, I talked to Agbayani. He had thought he would start the season with the Met farm team in Norfolk; now he was one of twenty-one Met players with absolutely no experience in a World Series, and was hungry to begin the games. He smiled and said that everybody on the team would be playing as hard as they could. "Hey, man," he said, "this is for the big cake." In that third game, played at Shea Stadium, the Mets won 4–2, thanks to a clutch double by Agbayani. Instantly, hope rose for millions of Met fans. Perhaps they might share some of the big cake too.

It was not to be, of course. But I felt an old-guy ache watching David Cone come out of the Yankee bullpen in Game 4. He was a fine pitcher for both the Mets and Yankees, but the season of the year 2000 had been a disaster. It was as if all his skills had vanished across one long summer. And here it was October, with two out in the fifth inning, and he had to face one batter: Mike Piazza, who had earlier hit a two-run homer. Cone got Piazza to pop up. The fine Met catcher might have been the last batter Cone would face in the major leagues. The Yankees won 3–2.

In Game 5, with a hazy fog rolling through chilly Shea, Al Leiter pitched with enormous skill and great heart. In the ninth inning, with the game tied 2–2, he struck out Tino Martinez and Paul O'Neill. Then he faced the catcher Jorge Posada. He appeared to have nipped him on a called strike three; the umpire called it a ball, and on the next pitch, Posada walked. Then Scott Brosius singled. The next hitter was a battered veteran with a lumpy body and a glorious face. His name was Luis Sojo. He hit Leiter's 142nd pitch of the night into center field for a base hit. A throw to the plate hit Posada in the back and rolled away, and here came Brosius in to score. It was now 4–2, Yankees. Leiter was done. And in the bottom of the ninth, with two out and a man on base, Mike Piazza came to bat. Mariano Rivera pitched. Piazza drove a long high ball into deep center field, where it seemed suspended for a few seconds in the fog. Then it fell into the hands of Bernie Williams just short of the warning track. A huge roar faded into a collective sigh. At the exact stroke of midnight, the Yankees had won their third straight World Series.

The details of this Subway Series will be argued by fans across the long winter. They will not discuss 1956 or 1947. And that's as it should be, because those years are now as remote to this time as the Spanish-American War was to my generation. But beyond the baseball, and beyond the final scores, there were many consolations, even for those of us cursed with memory and irony. For a few days in October, the Yankees and Mets gave some aging men and women reason to reflect without shame on the years when they were young. That was a gift. But the young people of the year 2000 were granted a gift too. The game of baseball gave them something they will remember for the rest of their lives: a Subway Series. That is, they were given another means of measuring time. And for five nights in the month of October, they were able to live for a while in a magical republic where everything seemed possible. Wait'll next year.

THE
SUBWAY SERIES
reader

MAYBE I REMEMBER
DIMAGGIO'S KICK

David Halberstam

LET ME BEGIN WITH A MEMORY. It was October 5, 1947, and I was in the Yankee Stadium bleachers, with the Yankees trailing 8–5 in the sixth. With two men on and two men out, Joe DiMaggio hit a tremendous drive to the deepest part of center field. A huge roar went up from the Yankee partisans in the bleachers, and then, as Al Gionfriddo made his celebrated catch, it seemed to ebb and turn into a gasp, while from the same section a second roar of approval exploded from the Dodger fans seated right there with us. Did I actually see the catch? I think I did. Did I see DiMaggio famously kick the dirt as he reached second, a moment replayed on countless television biographies of him because it was the rarest display of public emotion on his part? Again, I think I did. Who knows? Memory is often less about truth than about what we want it to be.

I think memories like this are critical to the current excitement in the city—baseball remains the most rooted of our sports and connects us to generations before, so that at a moment like this past and present merge. When I was young there were three teams in the city and all three were good. Since there were only sixteen teams in both leagues and only about four or five of them were actually competitive, a Subway Series for a time seemed something of a New Yorker's birthright. The last time two New York teams played in a Series, Dwight Eisenhower was running against Adlai Stevenson, the subway token was fifteen cents, and the door was just beginning to open for black and Hispanic players. In 1956 the Yankees, not exactly an affirmative action employer, were ever so timidly making their first accommodations to a more diverse sports world. Elston Howard had joined the club the year before. These days, on the occasion that El Duque pitches, the current Yankees will start as many as six players of black and Hispanic origin.

There was in those Octobers now past a great sense of celebration. A Subway Series helped New Yorkers do one of their favorite things—think about themselves. You could, in some of those years before television and air conditioning made their great strides forward, walk down the street in one of the boroughs, hear radios blasting out through open windows, and never miss a play.

It's all different now. If you get in a cab these days the odds are slim (it must be those foreigners that John Rocker was complaining about) that the driver will care about baseball. Today's players are bigger, stronger, faster, and much, much richer. Ballantine beer is gone, as are Old Gold cigarettes. Baseball no longer dominates the landscape of sports as it did. Because of television, by the late fifties and early sixties pro football was beginning to reach parity with pro baseball. But it's going to be fun here for about two weeks, and it's going to flood many of us with memories of what we will choose to think of as a simpler era and where we were on a given day when baseball ruled the city.

Normally getting just one team into a championship event serves to bring a community together, and people talk to each other about sports across the normal barriers of class, age, and ethnicity. A Subway Series is slightly different; it both unites and divides. Right now the city seems quite pleasantly wired for the event: after all, there's nothing more exciting than a war within a family, which in a way this is.

On a brief poll on our block, I find a doorman and a super who are for the Yankees and a doorman and a super who are for the Mets. In our building, Ralph Thomas, who runs the elevator, is, I think, covertly for the Mets, but he's quite low-key about it because he knows that Jeff and Linda Drogin and I are Yankee fans.

The crowds will be noisier than in the past—there's less civility at the ballpark because there's less civility in the society. The networks may be worried about the lack of geographic diversity and its effect on ratings. The rest of the nation will probably be underwhelmed. After all, much of America, for reasons that continually perplex most New Yorkers, sees us as loud, noisy, and aggressive, above all insensitive to the nuances and pleasures and culture of other places. That is, the rest of the country sees New York much the way the rest of the world sees America. Both teams seem to me very good, well balanced with good pitching. If anything, the Mets have been playing better all-around baseball for the last six weeks. But I'll go with my roots. The first game I remember hearing was in 1941, when Mickey Owen dropped strike 3 on Tommy Henrich and we still lived in the Bronx at the Grand Concourse and 174th Street. Rooting for the Yankees, it seems, is in my gene pool. Besides, I like Joe Torre. He's as decent and wise a man as I've met in professional sports. The Yankees in six or seven.

DAVID HALBERSTAM was the editor, with Glen Stout, of *The Best American Sports Writing of the Century.*

THE VOYAGE OF
SKIPPER BILL

LAWRENCE S. RITTER

The Subway Series of 2000 dragged me back in time exactly sixty-four years to my first one—Giants vs. Yankees—in 1936. Specifically, my thoughts returned to the second game of that Series. The economy was in depression then, big time, and the Subway Series—the first since 1923—gave New Yorkers something to take their minds off their troubles.

I was a seventeen-year-old New York Giants fan in 1936, living at home in Hollis, Queens. As October approached, I was hopeful, although a touch apprehensive. I realized that the Yankees had a good team, good enough to finish the season all of 19½ games ahead of the second-place Detroit Tigers. Babe Ruth had retired in 1935, but the Yankees still had Lou Gehrig, now the league leader in home runs, at first base, "Poosh 'em Up" Tony Lazzeri at second, Bill Dickey behind the plate, and a rookie named Joe DiMaggio in center field.

Nevertheless, I was sure my Giants were better.

Led by playing manager Bill Terry, still the National League's last .400 hitter (.401 in 1930), we also had Ott and Hubbell. Mel Ott in right field had led *his* league in home runs, and left-handed screwballer Carl Hubbell hadn't lost a game since the middle of July. As the regular season came to a close, Hubbell's open-ended winning streak had reached 16.

This past summer I was rudely yanked back to 1936 when a research-oriented friend sent me a copy of a venerable newsletter, *Giants Jottings*, a monthly fan-oriented periodical published in the thirties by the Giants. This particular issue was dated September 5, 1936, and an arrow in red crayon pointed to a letter in a section headed "Voice of the Fans":

To the Editor:

Our Giants have been playing the best ball possible for the last few weeks and deserve the support of every fan in New York because of their great spirit. Congratulations to Skipper Bill and his valiant crew for some great work.

LARRY RITTER, *Hollis, L. I.*

Because of school, I was unable to make it to the first game of the World Series, which was played at the Polo Grounds. Behind Hubbell, the Giants won, 6–1, giving rise to dreams of a sweep. Unfortunately, the second game was quite a different matter, a traumatic nightmare I still try to shake out of my mind.

To get to my favorite seat in the center-field bleachers, I arrived at the Polo Grounds at six A.M. on the morning of October 2. The game would not start until mid-afternoon, but the gates opened at nine A.M., first come first served, because the bleachers had no reserved seats.

The bleachers at the Polo Grounds were no bargain because they were so far from the action. Only kids with keen eyesight or folks with binoculars could make out what was going on at home plate, 470 or more feet away. Which of course didn't prevent us from constantly second-guessing the home-plate umpire on balls and strikes!

Actually, there were *two* bleachers, one on the right-field side of the center-field clubhouse and the other on the left-field side. Traditionally, the Giants' locker room was in the right-field side of the clubhouse and the visiting team's in the left-field side. My favorite seat in the bleachers was on the left-field side, where I always tried to grab a spot directly above a large pedestrian entrance/exit so no one could stand up in front of me and obstruct my view.

With President Franklin Delano Roosevelt throwing out the ceremonial first ball—election day was only a month away—the starting pitchers were Lefty Gomez for the Yankees and Hal Schumacher for Skipper Bill's crew. The Yankees immediately scored two runs in the first inning and the Giants one in the second before reality unceremoniously intruded.

In the third inning, the Yankees scored three runs

before anyone was out and then, with the bases loaded, veteran Yankee second baseman Tony Lazzeri took all the fun out of life when he smashed a grand-slam home run into the lower right field grandstand. In the ninth inning, Bill Dickey hit a three-run homer in the same place. The final score was an embarrassing 18–4, the worst World Series defeat ever suffered before or since. (The Yankees, of course, went on to win the Series in six games, the last game another blowout, 13–5.)

With two down in the bottom of the ninth, Giants outfielder Hank Leiber launched a long fly ball to deep center field that Joe DiMaggio gathered in effortlessly; without breaking stride, he started to run up the club-house steps to the Yankees' locker room. Suddenly DiMaggio stopped and turned toward the infield. He had belatedly remembered that everyone had been asked to remain in the stands and on the field until the president and his entourage had departed.

As President Roosevelt's open limousine passed by us bleacherites and Joe DiMaggio on its way out of the Polo Grounds via the center-field exit, the president waved to us and saluted the center fielder, who stood at attention and saluted back with a military flourish. Then both men were gone, Roosevelt to Eighth Avenue and presumably downtown and DiMaggio to the Yankees' locker room and probably Toots Shor's.

I shuffled out of the Polo Grounds that fall day with mixed feelings. I was sad because my hero, Skipper Bill, and his doughty crew had suffered an igno-minious defeat. At the same time, I was thrilled that I had seen another of my heroes, the president of the United States, at such close quarters.

That was sixty-four years ago, and for some reason, I do not know why, everything that happened on that eventful afternoon is still as vivid in my mind as it was on October 2, 1936. Much has changed since then, but a lot has not: given the chance, I would still vote for FDR and root for Skipper Bill and his stouthearted crew.

Let's go, Mets!

LAWRENCE S. RITTER is professor emeritus of finance at New York University. He is the author of *The Glory of Their Times* and *Lost Ballparks* and coauthor of *The Sportswriter Loses Control*, a novel.

OH, SWELL.
NEW YORK WINS AGAIN

GEORGE WILL

ONLY IN AMERICA. In a year in which presidential politics is a Horatio Alger story, proving that a Yale-educated son of a president can grow up to run for president against a Harvard-educated son of a senator, the national pastime is proving that two teams from New York, each with a payroll the size of the GDP of a medium-size third world nation, can get to the World Series. Is this a great country or what?

Listen up, New York. Not that you, in your self-absorption, give a damn, but this is how the rest of us feel about your October party: A wit who disliked both Thomas Carlyle and Mrs. Carlyle said that it was good of God to arrange for the two of them to marry so that only two people instead of four would be made miserable. For America west of the Hudson, the best thing about a Subway Series is that it guarantees that millions of New York baseball fans—the followers of whichever team loses—are going to be depressed.

A Subway Series is particularly galling to us gee-zers who were growing up embittered when, from 1949 through 1953, the Yankees won all five Series. In 1949, 1952, and 1953 they played the Dodgers. In 1951 they played the Giants, who played in the Polo Grounds, just across the Harlem River from Yankee Stadium. (In 1951 all three New York teams finished first: the Dodgers and Giants tied, and the Giants won the playoff on Bobby Thomson's home run.) What happened in 1950 that prevented every game of five consecutive Series being played in New York? This happened:

The Philadelphia Phillies, who had been in only one World Series (in 1915, which they lost), suffered a September swoon, shrinking their nine-game lead over the Dodgers, and they were limping. The Phillies lost seven of nine; the Dodgers won twelve of fifteen and trailed the Phillies by just two with two games to play, in Brooklyn. The Phillies lost the first. If they lost the last one, they would face a three-game playoff against the sizzling Dodgers.

The score was 1–1 in the bottom of the ninth when Cal Abrams reached second with no one out. Robin Roberts pitched to Duke Snider, who scorched a single to center fielder Richie Ashburn, like Roberts and Snider a future Hall of Famer. Ashburn could run like a whippet and played shallow. He fielded Snider's hit on the first bounce. The Dodgers' third-base coach waved Abrams around third. Abrams was out by a country mile. The Phillies won in the tenth. But had Abrams been held at third, with Jackie Robinson, Carl Furillo, and Gil Hodges due up, the Dodgers probably would have won, and probably would have whomped the sagging Phillies in the playoff. In the Series, the Yankees swept the Phillies.

But for that third-base coach's mistake (for which he was fired), no Series game after 1948 and before 1954 would have been played outside a circle with a seven-mile radius. In 1954 the Indians beat the Yankees by winning an American League record 111 games (in a 152-game season). If 103 wins (the 1954 Yankees total) had, as 103 almost always do, sufficed to earn a place in the Series, the Yankees would have been in six straight. Make that ten straight: they were in the 1955, 1956, 1957, and 1958 Series. They were also there in 1960, 1961, 1962, 1963, and 1964. In the twentieth century's ninety-five Series, more than half—forty-nine—included at least one New York team, and thirteen featured two. Thirty-three Series were won by New York teams—twenty-five by the Yankees. So now a new century begins and . . . yet again both Series teams are from New York. As has been said, history isn't one damn thing after another; it's the same damn thing over and over.

This year Payroll Number 1 (the Yankees' $114 million) battles Payroll Number 3 (the Mets' $99.8 million). Somehow Payroll Number 2 (the Dodgers' $105 million) managed to miss the postseason. The Yankees and Mets would not be where they are if the people running them did not have tremendous baseball acumen. But they also have huge advantages in local broadcast revenues. There is something amiss in baseball when so much is predictable just by counting the number of television sets in each team's market.

A few weeks ago I wrote about a report (submitted to baseball commissioner Bud Selig by Yale president Richard Levin, former senator George Mitchell, former Federal Reserve Board chairman Paul Volcker, and this columnist) concerning major league baseball's revenue disparities and competitive balance. The report documented that today's gargantuan revenue disparities produce ludicrous payroll disparities and competitive imbalance. The report noted that in the five seasons since the 1994 strike, there had been 158 postseason games, all won by teams in the top two payroll quartiles. And all World Series games had been won by teams in the top quartile.

Critics of the report noted this year's successes of the A's (the 23rd largest payroll), White Sox (24th), and Giants (18th). Well. Their combined postseason record this year: three wins, nine losses. Depending on whether this year's Series goes four, five, six, or seven games, teams in the top two quartiles will have won between 185 and 188 postseason games since 1994, those in the bottom two quartiles only three.

Now, one does not want to be a wet blanket at baseball's movable feast, the Series. Both the Yankees and Mets are gallant competitors, blending youth and age and featuring at least four probable future Hall of Famers (Mike Piazza, Derek Jeter, Roger Clemens, Joe Torre, and perhaps John Franco, Bernie Williams, and Mariano Rivera, too). Arguably, the Yankee dynasty is, on balance, beneficial to baseball. If there's no Goliath, there is no way for Davids to prove their pluck. And the trains (yes, children, there were such things) that brought the Yankees to St. Louis brought a reason to buy a ticket to see the Browns (yes, children, there was such a team). Besides, the two best teams are supposed to get to the Series, and this year they seem to have. One more thing: a Subway Series encourages New Yorkers to vent their native rudeness on each other rather than on the rest of us.

GEORGE WILL is the author of *Men at Work* and *Bunts,* and a regular columnist for *Newsweek.*

STILL WAITING

WILFRID SHEED

THE FIRST TIME THE Brooklyn Dodgers broke my heart, I hadn't even seen them play yet, or, truth be told, discovered exactly where Brooklyn was either. As a ten-year-old war refugee, stranded some hundred miles from the nearest New York subway, I used to while away the boiling afternoons of August 1941 by spinning the dial of our grandfather radio, which offered a choice of either listening to the nearby Philadelphia Phillies and Athletics take turns losing, or to this other team winning.

So I enrolled bit by bit, and without ever exactly knowing it, as an outpatient in the Red Barber wing of the Brooklyn Dodger nuthouse. Well, the man did have a nice voice, tailor-made for long hot afternoons and for selling stuff at kitchen doors, and in no time he had made me a rabid fan of Wheaties breakfast cereal (and of Old Gold cigarettes too, if I could ever get my little hands on a pack).

And besides, this seemed to be a pretty exciting team he was selling, hysterically so by Philadelphia standards. Leo Durocher tended to manage in the style of the Clanton brothers bursting into a bar looking for Wyatt Earp, while his henchmen Ducky Medwick and "Pistol Pete" Reiser took playful potshots at the whiskey bottles and the customers' boots. After a Dodger game, win or lose, you felt that something had happened. You had, for better or worse, *lived.*

On the whole, I probably would have been better off playing house with a pet boa constrictor, because by the time the season had ended, to all intents, with Mickey Owen dropping that crazy third strike in the first Yankee-Dodger World Series, I was hooked for life, without appeal or parole, on a team that doesn't even exist anymore, but which still sends messages every fall. "Beat those creeps this year, and let my soul catch some rest around here, for chrissake."

The radio was a huge part of it, much huger than television would ever be, because it caught the pauses better, and the stillness at the heart of baseball. Even in those days, the fat cats had begun to replace the real fans in the good seats anyway, and were beginning to eye the bad seats too, so that a lot more people already went to the game by radio than by subway.

You didn't have to go far, or even to stay in one place, to do this. Every store obligingly had its door open and every car window was down, so you could follow each inning on a sequence of blaring radios without breaking stride in your shopping or whatever, and carry on a running conversation about it with a hundred warm personal strangers along the way.

And that was just in Manhattan, the melting pot of the boroughs, to which we moved a couple of years later. For Brooklyn, you had to double everything. But there were Dodger fans everywhere, and they got lots of practice talking because by fall, they had already had their real Subway Series, without benefit of fat cats, in the form of twenty-two mouthwatering games against the New York Giants, each of which brought both teams' fans roaring onto the street, while the Yankee supporters presumably sat alone in their penthouses feeding their orchids and their parakeets.

Or so we imagined. In those days, the team images were as much a part of the mystique and the fun as the donkeys and elephants of politics. The basic Dodger was a stubbly old bum holding his cigar butt by a toothpick with all the panache of FDR waving his cigarette holder; the Giant was Old New York, Diamond Jim Brady in all his finery, a dandy from another age; and the Yankee was a banker in striped pants, dispossessing your relatives *right now* as he smothered his yawns and checked his stock prices.

These images would limp their way into the television era, but only just, because we see the players themselves every day now and real faces began to take over from cartoons, in particular the faces of Mantle,

Berra, and Whitey Ford on their side and Snider, Campy, and Jackie Robinson on ours.

These guys at least looked human, and surely we had a chance against humans. So why couldn't we win? The Yankees of the thirties and forties had always seemed to come from another planet anyway, where they did things better, and they could beat you half to death with their reputation and their press clippings before the first pitch was thrown. As Muhammad Ali once said of a kick boxer who challenged him, "He's heard a lot more about me than I have about him," and a legend can whip a nonentity any time.

But we *knew* these guys now; we played them every year. So what was the problem? As the 1950s moved along, awe and stage fright gave way rapidly to blind frustration. One year, a least likely suspect like Gil Hodges would go into a killer slump, and the next a stumblebum like Billy Martin would catch unprecedented fire, and *every* year the Dodgers seemed to come up one pitcher short. Punchy from watching home runs fly out of their child-size home park, and without a travel date allowed in those days to recoup—well, never mind all the excuses we made for our pitching. One year Don Newcombe was away in the army, the next he unfortunately wasn't. And so it went.

Fortunately we didn't need any excuses at all in 1955, the year with the golden asterisk when the Yankees stumbled into a patch of Kryptonite and we actually got to play some ball with them. But then in 1956, we learned that excuses had nothing to do with it in the first place. If the Wild Man of Borneo himself, Don Larsen, could draw an umpire blind or kind enough to grant him a perfect game, then this whole thing was out of our hands. We might think these guys were human, but they were really the same old New York Yankees, and they could still foreclose on bums like us any time their cold hearts chose.

And there the matter rested for the next forty-four years. In 1957 the Bums decided to try their luck in Hollywood, and the Giants escaped from old New York to old San Francisco, and even the Yankees took to losing every second World Series or so for a while before almost slipping off the map completely for a decade or two. And the memories got fainter and less painful—well, a little less painful. And that, we had every reason to hope, was that.

But new millennia call for new stories and here we were again this year with brand new players and presumably new scripts. The Dodgers and Giants had been replaced by a team called the New York Mets which had already clawed and scratched out its own little history unburdened by ancient curses and recurrent nightmares.

By the year 2000, America had eliminated ghosts anyway, and everybody knew everything there was to know about everybody else. And what with free agents and interleague play, there was no such thing as a Yankee mystique anymore, or any other kind of mystique. Their uppity fans had long since come down from the boardroom and were now just as noisy and vulgar as ours. And as final proof of their new humility and fallibility, the players themselves now accepted victory parades in their honor, as if victory was something special. The great Yankee teams of the DiMaggio era could hardly be bothered to hang around for even a small postgame celebration in the clubhouse—not if the duck hunting season had started, or the tarpon were biting off the coast of Cuba.

And yet and yet. Again we made the mistakes and they didn't. And the Yankees seemed to get one more run per game than they deserved and the Mets one fewer, and in no time we heard the familiar words "Yankees in five," which was where I had come in over half a century earlier.

The only difference, so far as I was concerned, was that I expected it to hurt as much as it always had but it didn't hurt at all. Maybe the new millennium was not going to be so different after all. At the age of roughly a hundred and fifty, baseball-time, I guess it's good to know that something, *anything*, hasn't changed, and I found myself fondly remembering all the other years when I'd heard those words, Yankees in five, six, or seven (they never swept us, thank God), and how much fun I'd had on the old Brooklyn Dodger roller coaster, reaching the sky in September and crashing down again in October, and signing up immediately for the next ride.

In fact, we even had a formula to see us through the long winter-waits between times, a phrase that was coined by chance in that same fateful year of 1941 and gives just as much comfort today as it did then. "Wait till next year," said the headline in the New York *Daily News,* and no one has ever had to say it again.

And this time we really mean it.

———————

WILFRID SHEED's books include *My Life as a Fan* and *Baseball and Lesser Sports.*

———————

SO MUCH MORE OF EVERYTHING

YOGI BERRA

I WAS LUCKY ENOUGH TO PLAY in fourteen World Series, and seven of them were Subway Series. Those were the really memorable ones. They had a holiday atmosphere, and it was so exciting everywhere you went. They were fun, too, because they were right here—you didn't have to travel far. We took a bus right from the Stadium to Ebbets Field, took just twenty minutes. It was great. There were about ten newspapers in New York, and they analyzed and covered everything. We also had hundreds of out-of-town writers, just like today, though today you also have those TV crews all over the place. The Series with the Yankees and Mets brought back a lot of memories, especially since people keep asking me all the time to compare them.

The big thing is the fans. To Yankee and Dodger fans, it was like a war. To us, it was a great rivalry, and we hated those guys on the field, but we were friends in the off season. I got to know Pee Wee, Campy, Jackie, and Branca pretty good—we went barnstorming with them in Japan, and they were great guys. Heck, I later coached for Gil Hodges with the Mets— we always had great respect for each other.

We had something like 74,000 fans at the Stadium for my very first World Series game in 1947. The Dodgers drew less than half of that because Ebbets Field was such a bandbox. I was just a twenty-two-year-old kid, a rookie. I was also pretty nervous. I'd never seen so much more of everything—more reporters, celebrities, politicians, cops, even umpires. (There were six umpires—I think this was the first World Series they ever used more than four.)

It was a real exciting World Series, that's for sure. I actually took the subway to one of the games with Frank Shea. We were single then, living in the Edison Hotel, so we figured it would be a good way to go. Frank was kind of a comic and he wore a mask on the subway so nobody would recognize him. He won the Series for us—he had a tremendous year for a rookie.

My performance wasn't so great. I wasn't a good catcher then. This was before Bill Dickey worked with me. My positioning was lousy, my throwing was lousy, and the Dodgers ran a lot off me. Connie Mack later said he never saw such lousy catching in his life. That was real nice.

I didn't catch all the games, and that wasn't all bad. In the third game, I hit the first World Series pinch homer ever. Everyone always remembers Larsen's perfect game in 1956, but we should've had the first no-hitter nine years earlier. Bill Bevens should've had one in Game 4. I felt real bad he didn't, and I felt even worse that we lost. Bevens was wild, but he had great stuff. I think he had ten walks, but nobody could hit him. In the ninth inning, we're up 1–0. He got the first out, then walked Furillo, but got Spider Jorgensen to pop up. One out to go. Al Gionfriddo ran for Furillo, and he broke for second; my throw was a little high, and the ump called him safe, although Rizzuto always insisted he was out. That shoulda been the no-hitter right there. Then Bevens walks another and Lavagetto hits one off the wall in right—game over. That was tough.

We bounced back and won the Series in seven, and we had a huge celebration. We even had a big parade in New York—the only time we ever had a parade. Even when we won those five straight (1949–53), we never got a parade. But those Series were all great fun. The Dodgers were a real strong club, they always had us on the ropes. But we always managed to win, except for '55—I always teased Pee Wee that we let them win that one.

Playing the Giants in 1951 was real intense, too. There was a lot of excitement, especially after Bobby Thomson hit that unbelievable homer. Some people said the Subway Series that year was like an anticlimax, but we sure didn't see it that way. A few of us actually went to the Polo Grounds for that last playoff game against the Dodgers, to see who we'd play in the Series. We left around the eighth inning, figuring we'd beat the crowd, and we listened to the rest on radio. We were on the George Washington Bridge when Thomson homered off Branca—I remember Russ Hodges going crazy. I guess the Giants proved what I always said: that it ain't over 'til it's over.

The Polo Grounds was just across the river from us, and that ballpark was old, shaped like a bathtub. It was okay, but it definitely wasn't the best place I ever played. The fans there were real loud, just like at Ebbets, and the Giants had the momentum; they were real confident, and everyone thought we were in trouble. It kind of looked that way for a while, too. This was DiMaggio's last year and he was hurting. Then Mickey ripped up his knee in Game 2, and Stanky kicked the ball out of Rizzuto's glove in Game 3. We were down two games to one and things didn't look real good. But then it rained the next day, so we got a day off and sort of regrouped. Eddie Lopat pitched two real strong games and Gil McDougald hit a big grand slam. We had the experience and depth—I think that was the difference. We won in six, and didn't play the Giants again in the World Series until 1962, when they were in San Francisco. That was a tough Series and we won. But they weren't our neighbors anymore.

My best memory was the '56 Series. Larsen's perfect game was one of the biggest thrills of my life.

Again, I wasn't as concerned with the perfect game as I was with winning it. The series was tied 2–2 and we only had a 2–0 lead going into the ninth. I remember Larsen never shaking me off, making great pitches all day—he only went to three balls on one guy, to Pee Wee in the first. That last inning was pretty tense. Furillo led off the ninth. I always liked talking to the hitters, and as he stepped in, I said, "This guy's got good stuff, huh?" He kind of grunted, then flied out. Then Campy grounded out. Then came Dale Mitchell, another real good hitter. My wife, Carmen, was in the stands, seven months pregnant. She promised if he made the final out, she'd name the baby after him—and that's why my youngest son is named Dale. We got Mitchell to strike out—yes, it was a strike. Some people say it was outside, but it was right on the corner. Even Mitchell said it didn't matter, he couldn't hit the strikes Larsen was throwing anyway.

I jumped into Larsen's arms, and it was a great feeling. Like I said, it had never happened before in World Series history, and it hasn't happened since.

Then Clem Labine pitched a great Game 6 for them, so it came down to another Game 7. I think people expected the Dodgers to win. They had Newcombe, who won twenty-seven games that year, while we had Johnny Kucks, who was just in his second year. He didn't even know he was going to start until he found the baseball in his shoe in his locker, which was how they let the starting pitcher know he was going to start that day. Johnny said he was thinking of putting the ball in somebody else's shoe, but he did just fine. He let two guys get on in the first, but then we got out of it with a double play, and after that he shut them down real good, pitching a three-hitter. I hit two homers off Newcombe, in the first and third, to give us a 4–0 lead. I actually felt a little bad for him. When Newk got up in the third inning, I told him he'd made a real good pitch, a low outside fastball, but I happened to get it good. I don't think that was any great consolation. We won, 9–0. I would've won the car they gave the MVP, but Larsen got it for making history. It was a Corvette, I think.

Nobody knew that would be the last Subway Series game, at least for a long time. It was Jackie's last game. It was also the last World Series game at Ebbets Field. It was sad when the Dodgers and Giants moved out west—they were so much a part of New York. I was lucky to be a Yankee, to play on great teams. I had great teammates, guys always pulling for each other. That's what these Yankees today remind me of. The fans in New York are the best anywhere—that's what makes a Subway Series so great. It's great for New York, great for baseball. I hope there's another one next year.

YOGI BERRA is a Hall of Famer and three-time MVP who played and managed for both the Yankees and the Mets.

THE THEOLOGY OF THE NEW YORK METS

RICK MOODY

TO BE A MET FAN, LIFELONG, is to be preoccupied with underdogs, and therefore to love and doubt equally. I inherited the tendency from my grandfather, a father-less soda jerk who rose to become the publisher of the New York *Daily News*, a newspaper that in 1969 had a large readership in the borough of Queens, the bor-ough that houses our beloved Shea Stadium. Because the New York *Daily News* had a Queens readership, the paper took a passionate interest in the 1969 World Series. Around our house, there were buttons and posters in profusion. I wore my Miracle Mets button to elementary school. As the Catholic schoolkid sports his or her crucifix.

The Mets never should have won the 1969 series. They lacked history, they lacked glamour, they'd pretty recently had the worst record ever in baseball. A black cat marched onto the field during one of their September games, or so I have heard. Same was true of the 1973 playoffs: The Mets should never have won. When the Mets were victorious back then, there was always the hair-raising probability of failure, the likelihood of a hideous mistake that would cost everything—and then, miraculously, success! Tug McGraw's famous formulation, *Ya Gotta Believe*, composed during this bygone era, is therefore not a remark about what a boost it is for ballplayers if the fans participate, but a confession of the possibility of baseball-related *despair*, which is always right around the corner. *Ya Gotta Believe*, that is, *against all doubt.* You don't need to believe in something assured. You don't need to believe, for example, in the New York Yankees, because the conclusion of a World Series involving the New York Yankees is never in doubt. At least not recently. You don't need to believe in Halley's comet or in full tide or in the bellicosity of politicians. *Ya Gotta Believe* only in what might be impossible. Therefore, when Tug McGraw invites your belief, he's saying, *We all know what it is to be human, how perfection is fleeting, how baseball is unpredictable, but we're asking you to look into your hearts and dream!* It's the sort of plea that will always persuade the sentimental baseball fan.

Neither, in 1986, did the Mets look to be in very good shape. The playoffs had their share of terrifying extra-inning exploits, as most of us will remember. However, I recollect the period sketchily because that October coincides with the end of my binge-drinking days. The Mets in October engendered a lot of late nights in bars with fans of dubious temperament, and yet, when everything should have gone wrong, *things nonetheless went right*, in both the playoffs and the World Series. Wally Backman kicked a ball and it stayed fair. Ray Knight dove and stopped a line drive. Mookie Wilson hit a dribbling single that any idiot (notwithstanding Bill Buckner) could have caught, and landed on first base. This part of the story is good. It's like when the Catholic church finally kicks ass in the Crusades. Everybody's happy. Jerusalem is rescued from the Infidel. However, we recognize this now as juvenile theology. You would find it easy to be an adherent of any *religion* that ensured parking spaces and a lifetime without income-tax audits—and yet in this blissful state you would not be experiencing *the bittersweet truth*.

The 1986 series was not what made the Mets a great and honorable baseball team. I can tell you this, because, as a binge drinker in certain sports bars of midtown, I took a misshapen pleasure out of the 1986 Mets. I was riled, screaming, wanting to tip things over. I was accosting strangers, and I didn't understand, as some of the cocaine-beguiled players on the team also did not understand, what was to happen next. What happened next was some *pretty good play*, in 1988, followed by uninspired playoffs, followed by a long interval of mediocrity. An interval of desperate trades (Bret Saberhagen, Bobby Bonilla) with minimal impact. An interval of drug rehabilitation and smoking in the dugout. An interval of underachievement, disappointment.

These are the days that make a true believer. Doubt is what creates a Mets fan. Ours is an existentialist theology, a theology of lack and want. As Met fans, we feel deeply the paradoxes of the Tao. Ours is an ecumenical theology that believes in heaven, *since we've already been through hell.*

Which brings us to the jubilee year, of course, the year 2000. Which brings us to the now traditional September Swoon, loss after loss after loss, gifted men batting .150, and so forth. Likewise, a complete failure of confidence when the team from Shea is faced with the Atlanta Braves or, in interleague play, the New York Yankees. This should come as no surprise. Terror is what afflicts doubters when they are faced with monolithic *certainty.* As when John Henry, looking around a bend in the tracks, perceives the steam train gaining on him. Those baseball teams that rely on the *purchasing power* of their ownership, viz the Atlanta Braves and the New York Yankees, are first corporate entities, rather than collections of *people;* or, if you prefer more theology, they are fundamentalists, literalists, admitting of no vacillation, no errancy. Accordingly, the best World Series of all would pit one of these steam-engine franchises against the doubting, human, frequently self-destructive New York Mets.

When we say that *Ya Gotta Believe,* therefore,

what is the term of license of our belief? Do we abandon the New York Mets when faced with the villainy and superior performance of a Roger Clemens? Do we shrink from the apparently unhittable Mariano Rivera? Do we avoid pitching to a preternatural Paul O'Neill as he bats .500 in the series? We do not. We welcome failure, as preliminary to spiritual growth. (It's part of being *ultimately concerned,* as Paul Tillich says.) The polar epicenters of the Mets' *spiritual victory over the 2000 Yankees,* therefore, are revealed in two spectacular moments during the Subway Series. First, in Game 2, during the famous *bat-throwing incident.* The moment to which I direct your attention comes to pass when Mike Piazza, lumbering up the first-base line, sees a chunk of his own bat (like a fragment of the true cross!) cartwheeling across his path, flung before him. His trot slows, he stops, *he turns.* Standing on the base line, waiting to see what will come of the moment, Piazza is neither villain nor hero (though he seemed heroic, three months prior, laid out flat in the batter's box, in the aftermath of his Roger Clemens concussion), but a *man,* one who knows his limitations, who trusts, who believes, who presents the other cheek. The baseball pragmatist will suggest that the Mets' inability to establish momentum in the Subway Series had to do with their failure to inflict like damage, after this martyrdom, on the person of some Yankee, on Derek Jeter or Bernie Williams, in recompense. But this is Old Testament theology, and has no place in the humanism of a sublime instant.

The other epiphany, *here in the Jubilee year,* comes in the person of Al Leiter, certainly one of the most personable and splendid of New York athletes of recent years. Doubters and deniers and blasphemers will spend months wondering why Bobby Valentine didn't *take Leiter out,* in the ninth inning of Game 5, before he gave up the series-winning runs to the unstoppable Yankees. But his ninth-inning collapse teaches us so much! Leiter's expressions and body language on the mound, comic, bizarre, outsized, reach a peak of woe and remorse after the Yankee runners score. He is an athlete, a competitor, a man completely responsible for his own failure, and he is displaying perfectly what the word *graceful* means. The Mets, as exemplars of human frailty, *had* to lose this year, and they had to lose to the Yankee machine, and we had to see Al Leiter suffer, in order to validate an important piece of ancient skepticism: *Except ye see signs and wonders, ye will not believe.* Failure and frailty and tragedy are assured. In recollection: Benitez, with a bad knee, is like a bruise on the heart every time he emerges from the bullpen; Edgardo Alfonzo and Timo Perez, so commanding in the playoffs, are about as useful at the plate as the banners waving above the center-field fence; most valuable free agent, Mike Hampton, cannot handle the northeastern chill, blows grimly upon his palms. It's all true. And yet, still, *Ya Gotta Believe.*

The Met fan takes the long view.

————————

RICK MOODY is the author of the novels *The Ice Storm* and *Purple America* and, most recently, a collection of stories, *Demonology.*

————————

BECAUSE OF THE PITCHER'S EYES

FRANK McCOURT

IF HE'S AROUND, I would like Mike Scott, formerly of the Houston Astros, to know about this. I would like him to know that because of his eyes I am somewhat interested in baseball, that I even watched a whole game on television when the Yankees finally clinched the game that sent them to the Subway Series.

It was you, Mike, and this is how it happened.

♦ ♦ ♦ ♦

In October 1986, they were talking baseball at the Lion's Head bar in Greenwich Village—Vic Ziegel, Pete Hamill, Tommy Butler—experts. They always talked baseball in October, and I didn't care because I didn't know the difference between a bunt and an R.B.I. I had grown up in Ireland with soccer, hurling, Gaelic football, rugby—games that moved, man. I couldn't understand these American games, football and baseball, where they stopped for a conference every few minutes before they decided on the next move. Why couldn't they just get on with it? If they stopped like that in Limerick, things would be thrown—insults about the players' mothers, any object at hand.

The Experts—Ziegel, Hamill, Butler—would pause to check up on whatever game was on television. There was no way of knowing if they liked what they saw since they all seemed to have attended the same academy of inscrutability. Tommy Butler would refill my beer glass and remark on the nice day outside but you could see his heart wasn't in the weather, that he was glad to return to baseball. At other times we would talk about jazz or the state of the world, but this was October and I might as well have had a communicable disease.

I'd like to have joined The Experts as they summoned up ghosts of Octobers past, as they employed their remarkable memories to recall statistics and moves from games fifty years ago. Despite my ignorance of the game, its starting and stopping and gawking and tugging and chewing and spitting, I knew there was something in the air. You couldn't escape the headlines: the Mets were on the march and that, surely, is what lay below the surface of The Experts' priestly talks. The New York Mets.

But up there on the television a pair of eyes, the

deadliest eyes I'd ever seen, a gunslinger's eyes. I ask Tommy Butler, "Who's that?"

"Mike Scott, Houston Astros."

His face fills the screen and his stare is enough to scorch anything in its way. He's staring at the batter, or is it the catcher? How am I to know? I can't ask The Experts for fear there might be pity for my ignorance. The catcher's fingers move. Mike Scott's eyes say "no," and that's the moment of my conversion. He throws the ball and I don't care where it goes or what the other team is.

Oh, I thought. So that's what it's all about. From Mike Scott's eyes an intimation of why there had to be a stopping and a starting, an epiphany that in the next few weeks helped me understand the battle between the Boston Red Sox and the Mets.

Of course I wanted the Mets to win, and for a very simple reason: There were people I disliked who were Yankee fans, and I wanted them brought low. Of course I knew the Yankees weren't in the Series, but I had no doubt they were sneering at the Mets and rooting for the Red Sox. I wanted those Yankee fans to get their comeuppance.

Now it's different. I am still an ignorant baseball fan, though learning more and more from my wife, Ellen, who, I'm sorry to say, is a Yankee fan. We are to baseball what James Carville and Mary Matalin are to politics. She loves the glamour and high elegance of the Yankees. I admire the come-from-behind rough-and-tumble of the Mets.

To Mike Scott, wherever you are, thanks for the moment.

Warm wishes to my wife and her fellow Yankee fans, but remember what Shakespeare said: "Uneasy lies the head that wears a crown."

FRANK MCCOURT is the author of *Angela's Ashes* and *'Tis*.

A tragedy of efforts: Timo Perez pays the price for not running hard on Todd Zeile's liner off the top of the wall as he's tagged out by Jorge Posada in the sixth inning of Game 1. *(AP Photo/Bill Kostroun)*

GAME 1:
BOTTOM OF THE NINTH

MIKE LUPICA

THE CITY HAD WAITED forty-four years for another Subway Series, and Mets fans had to feel they had waited twice as long for this kind of clear shot at the hated Yankees. Now the very first night had become a dream night for them at Yankee Stadium, because it had become a Met night, the Stadium filled with Met noise in the late innings. A Queens cheer in the Bronx. It was only Game One, but it felt like more to the Mets and their fans. Sometimes a great drama comes early in the World Series.

The Mets needed just two more outs. ("You can't run out the clock in baseball," Joe Torre would say. "You have to get twenty-seven outs.") The Yankees had been ahead, but then the Mets scored three runs in the seventh to make it 3–2. Armando Benitez, the Mets' closer, was in the game, replacing Johnny Franco of Brooklyn, who at the age of forty had just pitched a scoreless eighth, the first World Series inning of his life.

And suddenly a moment at the end of Game 1 was as important to this Subway Series as if this were Game 7. It happens that way sometimes. It happened that way when Kirk Gibson of the Dodgers hit a bottom-of-the-ninth, Game 1 home run against the Oakland A's in 1988. Jose Canseco, in the house now for the Yankees, had hit a grand slam that night for the A's and the A's had made those runs stand up until they asked Dennis Eckersley, then the best closer in the world, to get them the last three outs. Then Gibson, who wasn't even supposed to play, limped out on a ruined leg, one that would keep him out of the rest of that Series, and hit one of the most famous home runs in baseball history. The A's never recovered.

Another time, in another Game 1, this one in 1990, Eric Davis of the Reds hit a two-run homer in the first inning off the A's ace, Dave Stewart. The Reds weren't supposed to have a chance against the A's. Davis hit a bomb to dead center in Riverfront Stadium that nearly busted a television camera CBS had used for its pregame show. It was as if Davis had rushed across the ring like Mike Tyson did in those days and smacked the other guy before he even knew the fight had started. The Reds won the game, and ended up sweeping the Series.

Paul O'Neill, one of the leaders of the Yankees, played for the Reds in 1990. "Sometimes," O'Neill once said about the '90 Series, "one moment can change everything."

O'Neill, thirty-seven years old and looking every day of it in the playoffs, stepped in now against Armando Benitez in the bottom of the ninth, one out, nobody on, nothing happening for the Yankees. O'Neill was one of the last chances for the Yankees on this night. Even in Yankee Stadium, they could not rouse themselves to believe it was much of a chance. O'Neill had hit only .211 in the division series against the A's, and .250 in the American League Championship Series against the Mariners. He had managed one hit in this game, a single to center, so now O'Neill's batting average for this postseason was .238, with one extra-base hit, a double. The Yankee fans yelling for him to get a hit were the same Yankee fans who had been yelling for Joe Torre to take him out of the lineup. Torre wouldn't do it, though he moved O'Neill down in the batting order, even pinch-hit for him sometimes. There was an embarrassing moment in the Mariners Series the previous Sunday, when O'Neill was on his way to the plate in Safeco Field before they were able to get his attention from the Yankee dugout and alert him that Torre had decided to send up Glenallen Hill as a pinch hitter.

But this was the Series. In the past, in O'Neill's proud Yankee past, he had found a way to beat you in the World Series even when he was playing on one leg.

O'Neill took ball one from Benitez.

Watching the two of them, Franco thought to himself, *Don't be afraid to come in on this guy.*

For a month, stretching back into the regular season, O'Neill hadn't been able to get around on much of anything. It had started with a sore hip, and sometimes that's all it takes to turn a good swing into a bad one; good hitters will tell you that you get some kind of hitch in your swing and all of a sudden it's all the way into your DNA. Already people were wondering if this would be O'Neill's last season with the Yankees, even though O'Neill had been one of the players who changed everything at Yankee Stadium in the 1990s.

Swinging strike from O'Neill.

The count was 1–1.

O'Neill would be asked later if he had any kind of specific game plan against Benitez and he said, "Not to give in."

O'Neill took a called strike. One and two.

O'Neill fouled off a pitch away, then another one.

"Now come in," Franco muttered.

Ball two.

And suddenly Benitez was the one giving in to O'Neill, as if O'Neill were Kirk Gibson and some kind of danger to hit a ball out of the park, even if no one could remember the last time O'Neill had done that, or even hit a ball real hard. One extra-base hit in the postseason, batting average of .238.

Four years earlier, the first time Torre's Yankees won the World Series, against the Braves, O'Neill played the Series with what was essentially a torn thigh muscle. Somehow he kept going out there to play. When it was two games all and the bottom of the ninth in Game 5, the Yankees trying to hold on to a 1–0 lead, O'Neill was still in right field at Atlanta Fulton-County Stadium when Luis Polonia came up as a pinch hitter with two outs, a man on. Polonia was in the Yankee dugout now, a teammate of O'Neill's, getting ready to pinch-hit. That night in '96, he made a great swing against John Wetteland and hit a ball that seemed like a sure thing to make it all the way to the wall in right center. But O'Neill, running on that bum leg, somehow chased it down a few feet from the wall. When the ball and the game were in his glove, he threw a little fist into the padding of the outfield wall. It was not just the last out of the game, it was the last out of Atlanta Fulton-County Stadium, which would be torn down before the next baseball season. The Yankees won the Series in Yankee Stadium two nights later, and one of the sights you remembered was O'Neill, bracing himself on his good leg, jumping into the pile of Yankees in the infield, more a boy than any of them.

The count went to 3–2 in the Subway Series.

O'Neill fouled off the first 3–2 pitch Benitez threw him.

Don't get yourself out, he told himself.

He told himself what you tell yourself all the way back to Little League, when you first dream of moments like this one: *A walk's as good as a hit.*

He fouled off another outside pitch.

In the Mets dugout, somebody said, "Away, away, away, goddamit!"

Once, when Benitez was with the Orioles, he nearly started a baseball riot when he intentionally hit Tino Martinez, the Yankee first baseman, in the back with a fastball. Now, in the biggest moment of Benitez's baseball life, as important and defining a moment as there would be in this Subway Series, he wouldn't come anywhere near Paul O'Neill.

They were nine pitches into the at-bat. Now there was Yankee noise in Yankee Stadium, everybody on their feet, cheering for the player they had wanted to sit the hell down.

O'Neill walked on the tenth pitch.

The place exploded as if O'Neill had hit a home run. Then Polonia, the old Brave, the one beaten by O'Neill in the Series once, singled to right, and Jose Vizcaino singled to left. The Yankees tied the Mets in the ninth and finally beat them in the thirteenth on a hit from Vizcaino, No. 13. Over the rest of the World Series, Paul O'Neill would get eight more hits off Met pitching, including two triples. None would be more important than a bottom-of-the-ninth walk in

Game 1. On a night when two more outs might have changed everything for the Mets, Paul O'Neill was the toughest out in the world.

———

MIKE LUPICA is a columnist for the New York *Daily News* and a regular on ESPN's *The Sports Reporters*. His latest novel, *Bump and Run*, was published by Putnam the day after the Subway Series ended.

———

WHERE HAVE YOU GONE, JOEY PEPITONE?

PETER RICHMOND

WE WERE THE LOST GENERATION, huddled in the upper deck of the prefurbished stadium, adrift in the only doldrums the modern Yankees have ever known.

The most significant trade of the time was Peterson's family for Kekich's. Our only royalty was Pepitone. We were as familiar with the cityscape outside the park—the massive courthouse, the 4 train squealing its way uptown behind the center-field bleachers, the bright red and green "Buy DiNoto's Bread" ad painted on the apartment building above the IRT station platform behind left field—as we were with the action down on the field itself, so often did we have to avert our eyes from Jerry Kenney and Horace Clarke trying to turn the double play.

Our only sense of the glory of previous interboro clashes was a faint glow from the dying embers of past legends—but they furnished little warmth in the upper deck general admission seats on the nights when Dooley Womack was on the mound, with Steve Hamilton coming in from the bullpen.

For those of us born too late to have witnessed the old Subway Series, the 2000 Revival carried a special significance. And now that it's in the books, each of us will have particular memories to savor: Torre's tears; O'Neill's ninth-inning walk in the first game; Sojo's fifth-game winning single; Jeter's first-pitch home run in the fourth game, the serve-notice swat that effectively sealed the whole thing.

I, on the other hand, after being tempered and seasoned by thirty-five years in the Bronx, will remember this one in a more personal way: as the tournament that finally cured me of my team. As the World Series that freed me up to be a baseball fan again.

I hadn't seen it coming. Right up until the first pitch, I'd assumed all along that I'd be backing my boys, as I had when the opponents were the lightweights from San Diego, and the insufferably bland Braves. Surely, this time, as always, I'd be siding with Tino and Brosius and Andy P., good men all, men who night after night donned their uniforms proud pinstripe by proud pinstripe.

Yes, there was a likeability to the Mets, from Hampton's grit to the workaday-warrior feel of Ventura and Zeile. But Valentine the Unlikable set my nerves on edge, and owner Nelson Doubleday belonged in some men's club in the nineteenth century.

And their success in '69 and '73 had made our mausoleum in the Bronx all the more gloomy.

Then came Saturday night, and Pettitte went into his first windup against someone named Timo, a kid chewing gum in the batter's box, with his mouth open, wearing a tacky black uniform, and promptly struck him out—whereupon my heart thudded, or maybe simply skipped a beat, with the realization that . . . I'd wanted this Timo to get on base. Work a walk. Slap a single. I was rooting for the Mets. The pendulum had finally swung. I did not want to see another Yankee parade in the Canyon of Heroes this time. It was time for the other hometown team to take a ride downtown.

I was ready for previously unimaginable emotions. I could admire Jay Payton and appreciate Piazza and just about love Al Leiter, as engagingly mortal a man as ever climbed to the top of a pitching mound. I might even develop a fondness for the Shea-scape itself: the cereal-bowl-ness of it unchanged for nearly forty years, its tacky integrity proclaiming itself a bargain ballpark secure in its own time and place.

This strikes you as heresy, of course; a true baseball fan, goes the common wisdom, loves the uniform forever, no matter who wears it, no matter who owns the team, no matter where they play their games.

But isn't it otherwise? Isn't the true baseball fan

the one who can defy the tyranny of the uniform, shed the shackle of blind allegiance? Blind allegiance is what The Owner relies on, year in, year out, to fill the coffers, so he can cavalierly disregard tradition and get the funding to commit his own heresies. And there were many through the years. Well, what else would you call The Owner's signing of Don Gullett if not heresy? Which treason is worse: my rooting for the team from Queens, or The Owner recruiting all of our enemies for thirty years?

You remember Gullett. He beat us in the lopsided '76 series—then turned around and gladly accepted The Owner's dollars to don the pinstripes. The enemy ace on the Reds staff that slapped us down to earth barely seconds after we'd been floated to heaven on the back of Chambliss's fly-ball home run—now a Yankee!

One time could have been forgiven. But The Owner kept doing it. Tommy John beat him, and soon after—voilà! Tommy was a Yankee. Tiant, too.

This was not sport. This was something more insidious, more mean-spirited, more Orwellian: I knew, I knew with certainty, that The Owner was stockpiling the men who had once vanquished him not to improve his team, but to rewrite history, like Winston Smith in *1984:* "We didn't get beaten by Don Gullett or Tommy John or Luis Tiant. These men are New York Yankees. You must be mistaken."

He'd always been addicted to stockpiling everyone else's high-profile talent, from Catfish and Reggie through Winfield and Baylor, but this was part of the rules of the modern game; that was nothing more than bullying by checkbook.

But Boggs? And Justice? And Clemens? These were not just other teams' stars. These were the enemies' stars. It was sacrilegious.

Maybe, yes, it was better than Bill Sudakis and Roger Repoz and Jake Gibbs. But not by a lot.

I've had plenty of time to ponder my actions, and I am at peace with myself. I still like Brosius and Tino and Andy and Joe. I just don't have to pretend I care about the mighty Yankees.

I have wondered exactly what constituted the last straw: Was it when Neagle showed up, the man who'd pitched against us in a Series just a few years ago? Or was it Canseco?

And then I remembered: It wasn't the arrival of a player. It was the loss of an advertisement.

The pivotal moment had arrived unannounced when, a few years ago, taking my seat for a game in the Stadium, I glanced up at the apartment building beyond the left-field wall and sensed that something was different. It took me a few innings to figure it out, but then it hit me: the "Buy DiNoto's Bread" sign, fading for years but always visible, was finally gone. It had been painted over. The wall was bright white—a tangible piece of cityscape no longer. Just a billboard a-borning, readying for a new advertisement, to reap The Owner some new revenue.

Through all of the years, through all of the heresies, the DiNoto Bakery sign had remained: a beacon from the past, certifying that no matter how mercenary the owner, how clueless he was of the real rules of the game, no matter how often he hinted that he was going to move the team downtown or across the river to Jersey, there was still a bond between the blue-collar Bronx and its baseball team.

That was the beginning of the end. And so, finally, I was ready for a new beginning: a baseball fan reborn. I could watch the Subway Series as a fan, and root for the game.

PETER RICHMOND is a special contributor to *GQ* magazine and the author of *Ballpark: Camden Yards and the Building of an American Dream.*

YANKEES, GO HOME!

JOHN LEO

ARE YOU EXCITED ABOUT THE Subway Series between the Mets and the Yankees? No, of course you aren't. We who live here in the Big Apple are fully aware that the frenzy over this long-awaited matchup is somewhat muted in America's trans-Hudson region. Many of you probably wanted to see a team from one of the top provincial cities (St. Louis) or even one from a remote outpost on the very edge of American civilization (Seattle). But, hey, those teams lost, and you are stuck with two from New York. So we know what you are thinking. You are thinking the same thing you thought during the Iran/Iraq war: Isn't it a shame that both sides can't lose?

But there are sound reasons for you to care. One of the teams represents truth, justice, the American way, and underdogs everywhere. The other represents George Steinbrenner. Ridiculously rich people who live in Manhattan root for the Yankees. When they hear about a coming Subway Series, they scratch their heads and ask their doormen, "What's a subway?" The Mets are located in Queens, where real people predominate. Yankee fans don't even know where Queens is. Luckily, their chauffeurs do, or Yankee fans would never be able to reach either city airport.

Statistics tell the story. Federal number crunchers confirm that 62 percent of Yankee fan support comes from the richest 1 percent of taxpayers! As I believe Al Gore pointed out in one of the debates, the Yankees are the team of HMOs, Big Oil, and Big Tobacco. When not chortling over a Yankee demolition of some harmless American League opponent, Yankee fans spend a lot of time worrying about the unfairness of death taxes on estates as small as $10 million.

Mets fans, on the other hand, are members of working families. Lacking the foresight to inherit trust funds, they have actual jobs. They don't go to work in pinstripes, and they don't send their baseball team out in them, either. Unlike Yankee fans, they do not expect to win every year, and they don't throw tantrums or complain bitterly to their butlers in those off years when they don't win the pennant.

Rooting for the Yankees has the same excitement level as rooting for Merrill Lynch or betting that the sun will come up in the morning. The Yankees have a tradition of mindless competence. The Mets, on the other hand, have a vibrant tradition of scrappy incompetence.

The typical Yankee hero was Joe DiMaggio. Joe D. was graceful, aloof. He played with no noticeable emotion of any kind. Nobody ever saw DiMaggio dive for a fly ball. He didn't have to. He always got there in time to make the catch look easy.

This bland, boring, ho-hum, Hall of Fame style may be fine for the Yankees, but it is definitely not for the Mets. The classic Met is "Marvelous Marv" Throneberry, who was way more exciting than Di-Maggio. Marv couldn't run, hit, throw, or catch, but he fit pretty well into the Mets scheme of things. When asked why the Mets didn't get Throneberry a birthday cake, manager Casey Stengel said, "We were going to get him a cake, but we figured he'd drop it." Marv once hit a triple and was called out for neglecting to touch second base along the way. He was not the sort of player who made the same mistake twice. No, the next time he hit a triple, he was called out for failing to touch first and second bases. Stengel once said that the Mets "have shown me ways to lose that I never even knew existed."

We had Jimmie Piersall, who ran the bases backward to celebrate his 100th home run. We had excruciating players like Chris Cannizzaro ("the only defensive catcher who can't catch," Stengel said) and other outstanding nonfielders with famous nicknames like "Dr. Strangeglove" (Dick Stuart).

The Mets are much better now, but they retain that scrappy, unpredictable underdog tradition. Look at the Mets playoff heroes. We have Benny Agbayani, the Hawaiian left fielder who batted first for the Mets most of the year. He was surely the most roly-poly leadoff hitter in modern baseball. His batting stance is alarming. Watching him chase fly balls is nerve-racking. But he played like a major star during the playoffs, so true Mets fans scream his name at every opportunity. The fans scream for Timo Perez, too. He's a big favorite at Shea Stadium, though he's been a Met only since the beginning of September. Timo is from the Dominican Republic by way of Japan, where he played for the Hiroshima Carp. He is small and has little power. The Yankees would never have given him a tryout. But he absolutely wrecked the Giants and Cardinals during the playoffs.

When the Yankees faltered in July, they simply went out and ransacked other teams, buying seven or eight more zillionaire ballplayers. That's the Yankee way. The Mets do it by producing improbable heroes like Timo and Benny. So who are you going to root for? Real people like Timo and Benny, or Yankee automatons and Steinbrenner's wallet?

Remember, being a Yankee fan isn't a serious enough offense to come up at a confirmation hearing. It's merely a character flaw. Go Mets.

―――――

JOHN LEO is a regular columnist for *U.S. News & World Report.*

―――――

THE PLAY'S THE THING

ROBERT K. MASSIE

BASEBALL FOR ME IS A kind of grand-scale, mostly outdoor repertory theater: the same home team players appearing nightly in a new play. The plot is always different, the local heroes confront a constantly changing band of out-of-town villains, suspense builds as the drama progresses, every night brings a fresh denouement accompanied by intense gratification or despair, mostly gone by morning because there is another game to watch in just a few hours.

It took time to develop this perspective. For half my life, I knew and cared little about baseball. I grew up in the South during the thirties and early forties when major league baseball was a game played far away. In those days, the sixteen teams traveled around a circuit defined by the distances they could travel overnight by rail or bus. There were no teams in the West, the Southwest, or the South, and the major league games played closest to my house in Nashville,

Tennessee, happened in Cincinnati and St. Louis, too far away to inspire interest or loyalty. Television didn't exist and radio—if a local station broadcast the games, I didn't know or care—was inadequate to bring small boys indoors on a beautiful spring or summer afternoon. (Years later, when I read Bart Giamatti's essay *The Green Fields of the Mind* about the joy of listening to baseball on radio, I understood what he was talking about, but that kind of visual imagery in the mind usually presupposed an established loyalty to one of the teams on the field.)

In college in New England at the end of the forties, I found myself among young men who cared intensely about baseball. A roommate from Cleveland spent the April and May afternoons of 1949 following the Indians by radio, his face glowing when Bobby Feller or Lou Boudreau outperformed that day's opponents. During those years, a friend from Nashville, originally as ignorant of baseball as I, went to New York to watch the Giants play at the Polo Grounds. His love affair with that team survived their move to San Francisco and the difficulties of watching games played in a time zone three hours away. It continues today, fifty years later. Now, in November 2000, his team having been eliminated 3–1 in the first round of this year's playoffs, he still argues vehemently, "This year, the Giants were the best team in baseball."

I became a Yankees fan because of two of my children. Like most Americans, I knew that Babe Ruth, Lou Gehrig, Joe DiMaggio, Mickey Mantle, and Roger Maris were Yankee immortals, but I didn't know why. Then, in 1977, when my daughter Elizabeth was twelve, she began asking to watch Yankee games. The reason, it turned out, was shortstop Bucky Dent, who was movie-star handsome and had an interesting way of hitching up his pants as he stepped into the batter's box. Elizabeth watched and eventually I sat down to see what was going on. It was a good year—Reggie Jackson, Thurman Munson, Willie Randolph, Graig Nettles, Ron Guidry, Catfish Hunter, and Sparky Lyle—and before long I was hooked. Eventually, I saw the remarkable sixth and final game in the 1977 World Series when Reggie hit three home runs, each on the first pitch, off three different pitchers.

In the eighties, Elizabeth and I lost interest. Bucky and Reggie were gone, the Yankees were losing, and the bullying side of George Steinbrenner's personality put even the remarkable Don Mattingly in the shade. The football Giants fought their way into two Super Bowls, and three hours a week watching them win seemed a more gratifying and economical way to spend time than three hours devoted every night to watching the Yankees lose.

Enter Christopher. My son, an eight-and-a-half-year-old Yankee fan, has superior baseball genes from his mother's side. His grandfather, a childhood habitué of Ebbets Field, a literary biographer and retired professor of English at New York University, knows so much about baseball that his copy of the 2,733-page *Baseball Encyclopedia* lies mostly unopened. His aunt, a China scholar, watched the World Series in Beijing last month via Japanese television. Christopher's mother, who also brings our infant daughters to Yankee games, used baseball as a tool to convince him that reading and mathematics had practical value: how else could one relive yesterday's game in today's newspaper and figure won-lost statistics, standings, games behind, batting averages, and pitcher's earned-run average?

Christopher was only four in 1996 and didn't pay much attention to the World Series when the Yankees came back from losing the first two games and won the next four straight. He became a Yankee fan in 1998; he says he started to watch because I was watching, and I remember continuing to watch because he was sitting with me. We became addicts. He devoured the sports pages every morning before school, consulted his grandfather frequently by phone, and in no time at all knew far more about the game and the players—not just the Yankee players, but *all* the players in baseball—than I. What's a suicide squeeze? I know, sort of. How does a pitcher concoct a change-up? I forget. What was Manny Ramirez's batting average this year? I have no idea. Christopher *knows*.

The only part of the game to which I perhaps bring

more knowledge is in appreciating the qualities of the current Yankee manager. Christopher's judgment on Joe Torre is practical and succinct: "I hope he comes back." For me, however, watching Torre in the dugout between the inimitable Zimmer and the kindly Stottlemyre has been to see a real-life, particularly American hero of the kind that Spencer Tracy and John Wayne used to play on celluloid. Through good times and bad, Torre sits there, his face impassive, betraying emotion only when he takes an occasional sip of bottled water. I don't know how much Joe knows about NATO or what to do about the surplus, but I wish we could find a president who could project the same rock-like certainty that, in the end, if everyone plays hard and does his job, everything will be all right.

Onto this Yankee repertory stage, Christopher and I saw the Mets arriving a few weeks ago, not as villains, but as worthy, colorful, and dangerous challengers. If the Yankees had lost earlier in the playoffs, I, at least, wanted the Mets to win; Christopher preferred Seattle. Bobby Valentine has panache and I'm glad he'll be back next year, but I wish he'd cut down on the bubble gum. Mike Piazza has been splendid, as much for the way he dealt twice with the overwired Roger Clemens as for his work at and behind the plate. If the Mets sign A-Rod and the Yankees don't tinker too much with a team that has won three straight and four out of five, Christopher and I think it can happen again next year: two games at Shea, three at the Stadium, and two back at Shea. If necessary.

ROBERT K. MASSIE is the author of *Nicholas and Alexandra*, the Pulitzer Prize–winning *Peter the Great*, *Dreadnought*, and *The Romanovs: The Final Chapter*.

Mets slayer Roger Clemens prepares to hurl the stake that had once been part of Mike Piazza's bat into Piazza's path and the Mets' hearts. Jorge Posada is oblivious, but umpire Charlie Reliford is already heading toward Clemens. (*Francis Specker/The New York Post*)

GAME 2:
ADVANCED ROGEROLOGY

BOB RYAN

ON THE OFF CHANCE A tumbling object that was quite obviously not a baseball were to approach the mound, most any major league pitcher would skip nimbly out of harm's way. But let's say, for the sake or argument, that the pitcher did happen to snare said tumbling object. Would not the next obvious move be to toss whatever it was gently aside, say in the direction of a batboy, who would then dispose of it in some appropriate manner? In the second inning of Game 2 in the 2000 World Series, Roger Clemens threw a pitch to Mike Piazza that broke his bat in three pieces. The shattered barrel of the bat came bouncing toward the mound. Rather than hop out of the way—the pointed end representing a very dangerous projectile—Clemens fielded the bat by the rounded end. He then fired it overhand toward the sideline, missing Piazza by just a few feet.

Since that moment, there has been one question

on the minds of several million people: *What was Roger Clemens thinking?*

Stop right there. Anyone asking that question has already demonstrated by definition that he or she does not understand Roger Clemens. The Rogerologists of the world knew better. He *wasn't* thinking, at least not in any conventional baseball sense. Roger Clemens wasn't thinking then any more than he was thinking three and a half months earlier when he threw a fastball that hit that same Mike Piazza in the head. In both cases Roger Clemens was engaging in foolish and reckless behavior emanating from the fact that when this man takes the mound he does so in an abnormal frenzy more associated with contact sports such as football and hockey than with baseball. It is, in fact, easier to comprehend why Roger Clemens is the way he is on the mound if you can think of him not as a pitcher, but as a Dick Butkus–type linebacker or a Marty McSorley–style hockey goon.

Roger Clemens is neither an evil nor a stupid person. In a world of phonies and hypocrites galore, he is a great husband and a true world-class father. No man could honor his mother more. He answers many a charity bell. He lives by a very clear code. As far as his intelligence goes, he may not be Alistair Cooke, but he's no dummy, either. What gets him into trouble is his difficulty in expressing himself. When giving explanations for his actions, he does not complete many sentences; he circles around and around and he assumes that the listener knows many facts that have not been placed in evidence, or, if they have, were put there a very long time ago. One other problem: he doesn't like to tell the truth when he realizes it will embarrass him. But he knows what he knows, and one thing he knows is pitching. He long ago earned his Ph.D. in moundology.

In addition to his knowledge, he brings to the mound a very strong right arm and, to a degree seldom on display in modern baseball competition, a sheer ferocity that sometimes propels him to do things that most everyone else might consider to be irrational. Does this excuse his excesses? No, certainly not. It merely explains them. The Yankees were well aware of those excesses when they signed him. Joe Torre and Derek Jeter had each condemned him for past head-hunting transgressions. Nor was Jeter the only new teammate who had sworn vengeance on Clemens for what they felt were his mean-spirited actions on the mound. In Roger's mind, buzzing people inside is his way of asserting himself. He regards it as sound pitching strategy. He sees himself an heir to the Bob Gibson/Don Drysdale tradition. Keep in mind also that Clemens's idol was Nolan Ryan, and Ryan was a man who was willing to accept a hit batsman or two as the price of doing business.

What separates Clemens from the others is the mind-set he brings with him to the mound. You never heard Gibson, Drysdale, or Ryan talking about the need to get hold of their emotions. They did what they did naturally. You cannot imagine Bob Gibson, who operated with the cold-blooded efficiency of a hit man, explaining that he had to "go into a room by myself" to calm down after the first inning of a World Series game. Roger Clemens needs to work himself into a football-type lather. Think back to the day he was ejected by Terry Cooney in Game 4 of the 1990 ALCS. Over and above the foolishness of the incident itself—how could Clemens possibly risk ejection in such an important game?—there was the matter of the warrior-like eye black he had smeared under his eyes. It had nothing to do with the sun and its glare. It was Roger Clemens's way of psyching himself up for the game.

So what would make anyone think this guy is normal? He's not. He's Roger. This isn't Lefty Grove (even though Lefty was known to tear up jerseys and kick lockers). This isn't Early Wynn, of whom it was said he would brush back his grandmother. This isn't Sal (The Barber) Maglie. This isn't Gibson, Drysdale, or Ryan. This is Roger Clemens, who is in such a frenzy when he pitches that he does irrational things and then finds himself incapable of explaining them when the time comes. Yet this same frenzied gentleman refused to allow the uproar over his bat-tossing to deter him from the task at hand. He refocused himself strongly enough to pitch eight innings of two-hit, shutout ball, a performance that, when coupled with his one-hitter against Seattle in his previous start, represented the most overpowering back-to-back postseason outings since Jim Lonborg's one-hitter/three-hitter in the 1967 World Series. That is why people put up with Roger Clemens's eccentricities. Few people believed Roger when he said he thought the object bouncing toward him was a baseball, not a bat. Fewer still believed him when he said he didn't even know Piazza was on the baseline when he whipped the bat in his direction. Of course they didn't. They were framing his actions in the context of, well, a "normal" pitcher, and the last thing anyone could say about a man who has honored his own strikeout image by naming his four male offspring Koby, Kory, Kacy, and Kody is "normal." If you want Roger Clemens on your team, you are compelled to take the entire bizarre package.

BOB RYAN is a longtime columnist for *The Boston Globe.*

PERIPHERAL VISION

JOE KLEIN

IT's SUNDAY EVENING IN Portland, Oregon. It's chilly, and Al Gore is late. Gore is excruciating under the best of circumstances; waiting for Gore is beyond intolerable—especially on a day that began about 28 hours ago in Philadelphia, a day in which we press-slugs seemed to travel everywhere and nowhere in America: to a sterile mega-church service in Dallas, and then to a rainy rally in Albuquerque, and then to Portland. I have eaten six meals this day (three on the press plane); all were swill, except for the quesadillas in Albuquerque. And throughout, I have been thinking about only one thing: If Gore is on schedule and the Portland rally ends on time, maybe I'll get to see the last few innings of Clemens vs. Hampton.

That is, if Clemens isn't routed early.

Yes, yes. I'm a Met fan, always have been, even before there were Mets. I went to twenty games in 1962 (the team rewarded my loyalty by winning five of those games, which matched their .250 winning percentage for the year). I saw Marv Throneberry miss first and second base when he hit the triple; I saw Hank Aaron wrist-snap two home runs out of the Polo Grounds in the first game of a twi-night doubleheader the day I took my Spanish Regents. I carried a sign with my friend Neil at the first Banner Day ("The Bums Went Away But The Mets Will Stay"). I had an architect's rendering of Shea Stadium on my bedroom wall—five levels of seats! Yankee Stadium had only three! Who knew that modernity would turn out to be so dreadful? (I felt betrayed when one level proved to be not seats but press box. The Mets have taught me so much about life and art.)

So, after all these years, I have a killer instinct for the peripheral—which sort of comes with the territory for a Mets fan (being on the periphery, I have learned, is the spiritual opposite of being on the edge). All of which is to confess: I am not thinking of Clemens vs. Piazza. I am obsessing about Mike Hampton. I imagine him stroking a two-out single to right field, with the bases loaded, bottom of the first, and Clemens trudging off the mound, hurling his glove, kicking dirt. (I am so on the periphery that I've forgotten the game is at Yankee Stadium, and Hampton won't bat.) I am certain that Hampton will pitch a four-hit shutout, and we'll lose him to some other team in the off-season. Every victory yields defeat: part of the karmic price one pays for being born in the outer boroughs, whence most serious Met fans hail. The outer boroughs define periphera. Mike Hampton is just too regular, too American to appreciate creative peripherality. (Unlike Piazza, who has a Bensonhurst aspect, down to his pigheaded insistence on catching instead of playing first base.) Hampton will win the game . . . and then, sayonara. These are my thoughts, waiting for Gore.

But someone is calling my name.

Jim Warren of the *Chicago Tribune*. He's wearing a Yankee hat and he is smiling: A Yankee fan from Chicago? I thought Hillary Clinton was the only one. Turns out, he's from the Upper West Side. "You're not gonna believe this!" he says. "First inning. Piazza and Clemens! It's classic. Unbelievable." What, I ask. "I can't believe it," he says. *What?* "It's gonna be talked about forever."

And then he tells me.

"Is Clemens still alive?" I ask.

Alive and pitching, apparently. And, oh, by the way, the Yanks are winning. And Gore is now an hour late for no apparent reason; a November wind is whistling, two weeks early, through tallish pines. A really terrible deejay is trying to keep the crowd enthused by playing hockey-fan music: We will, we will rock you. The dregs of Freddie Mercury. (Okay, they play this garbage at Shea, too.) Every so often, Jim Warren materializes with an update. More bad news. The story of my life: we're falling further behind, and I can't even watch it.

Finally, Gore appears. Introduced by John Sweeney of the AFL-CIO, who looks and sounds like an outer-borough type—the father of one of the Irish kids who used to beat me up, which serves only to intensify my longing: baseball was a haven from the reality of the schoolyard. The Mets were a team for kids who got beat up. At one of my first Polo Grounds games, as we were being pummeled by the Cubs, I sat in front of a black man who was either drunk or just very sad. "My poor baby Mets," he keened, "my poor, poor baby Mets."

Sweeney delivers a long and graceless introduction, more evidence of the waning of trade unionism. Jim Warren sidles over. "Six–nothing." He pats me on the back. I do not tell him what he can do with his patronizing sympathy.

Finally, Gore. A woman begins to scream. I have never heard such screaming. She is screaming about something incomprehensible—but the words "lie" and "die" are involved. She's standing on a metal fence, leaning over it now, her mouth open so wide that it seems computer-animated—and then she launches herself over the fence, head first. The Secret Service swarms, pinioning her arms, cuffing her face-down on the ground (she's still screaming, muffled now). Gore seems distracted, or maybe it's just me. I really want to know what she's upset about. An odd, delicate moment transpires: a Secret Service fellow squats down next to her and begins whispering softly; I can't hear what he's saying, but it is obviously lovely and hypnotic. His balm is more fascinating than her anger. Both are better than Gore.

"I want to fight for you!" Gore is yelling.

Please don't, I am thinking. Don't fight. Just perorate.

Jim Warren again, looking pale now. I'd forgotten the game, given it up. Allowed my subconscious to drift back to Benitez-loathing, and the utter certainty that the Series had been kicked away, spiritually, in the first game.

"Six to five," Warren says, shaken.

"What inning?"

"Not sure," he says.

"It's over," an AP guy says, since AP guys always know everything first. "The Mets scored five runs in the ninth. But they lost."

A dull ache—a familiar ache; a reassuring pain, if such a thing is possible. I am at the Polo Grounds D train station, the tiles are black and orange, New York Giant colors. We have lost the twi-night doubleheader to the Braves, but I am optimistic. I am convinced that if Casey would only play Rod Kanehl—a fabulously peripheral figure, a utility infielder on the worst team in history (he had a couple of hits that day)—we'd do better. But that doesn't matter; I remember what a world without Mets was like, and this is better.

I celebrate our losses, I cherish our futility. I have a richer fantasy life, I have experienced more, I *know* more than most Yankee fans. And I can live with less.

—————

JOE KLEIN writes about politics for *The New Yorker,* and is the author of *Primary Colors* and *The Running Mate.*

—————

A SENSE OF
WHERE YOU AREN'T

BOB GREENE

THE REASON THE 2000 World Series got the lowest television ratings in Series history is not—as many New Yorkers believe—because the rest of the nation hates New York, and thus hates New York sports teams.

Hatred is good for television ratings. Hatred puts ratings through the roof.

No, the most hurtful emotion—as anyone who has ever been in love can tell you—is not hatred.

The most hurtful emotion is indifference.

And indifference is what most of America felt about the so-called Subway Series of 2000. The Yankees and the Mets could overcome a lot, but they could not overcome the indifference their countrymen and countrywomen felt about the five baseball games the two teams played in October.

To understand this—the reason for the indifference—you must start with the idea that the concept of "place," as we have always known it, has undergone a profound transformation.

New York was always the top place, the dreamed-of place, back when place meant something.

This is why, in the 1950s, people all across the United States would gather around their radios at work or at school on autumn afternoons to listen to the New York baseball teams play each other in the Series.

New York was . . .

Well, if you didn't live there, New York was grand almost beyond imagining. And the imagining was the key: New York was so wonderful (as in *Wonderful Town*) in the public imagination that if you had never been there, it was almost impossible to conjure the purported glory of what that experience would be like. New York, for those who had never seen it with their own eyes, was the New York of Frank Sinatra and Gene Kelly on shore leave . . . the New York of swelling, peppy, movie-soundtrack orchestral themes against a Technicolor Manhattan skyline . . . the New York where everything, even the smallest thing, seemed bigger in the telling. The Bronx is up and the Battery's down, indeed.

That's what made those radio broadcasts of the old-time Series more intoxicating than anything you could see. I remember, as a child in central Ohio, shooting baskets with my friends on the blacktop of the elementary school playground while a battery-powered radio a few feet away told us pitch by pitch what the Yankees and the Dodgers were doing. We were in the same time zone—Eastern—but New York might as well have been forty million miles from us. We could hear the voices in the crowds at Yankee Stadium, at Ebbets Field . . . but those voices could have been coming from a separate stratosphere. We could as easily imagine dancing on the rings of Saturn as sitting in the stands in Yankee Stadium.

That was before the concept of place was erased. That was before—with instantly televised live images inescapable on scores, even hundreds, of cable channels—the very meaning of a faraway place came to signify almost nothing. Grandeur? Mystique? Deleted. When you can summon before you anyplace in the world, on demand, and then click to some other place in a fraction of a sliver of a second, your senses are dulled, muted. Place? You see New York—and Los Angeles, and Moscow, and Paris, and Beirut—all the time. They're constant presences on your glass screens. The legendary cities might as well be your boring next-door neighbors.

The rallying mantra of the worldwide computer network is "Where Do You Want to Go Today?" We have all been sold on the premise that if we sit in our rooms and tap at a keyboard, we can be transported across the universe. We can go everywhere without going anywhere. We have accepted the premise; we have vowed to believe. Distance no longer means a thing. Anyplace in the world can be delivered to us faster than a pizza.

It should be no surprise, then, that when the 2000 Subway Series came to pass, there was not exactly mass swooning throughout the land. Two New York teams were going to play some games? It did not have quite the grip on the national imagination that the New York/New York Series did in those now-lost days of transistor balls and strikes on midwestern fall afternoons. In our new world in which everyone has seen everything, a live-as-it-transpires broadcast of Timbuktu vs. Istanbul would produce not much more than a chorus of yawns. People are expected to get worked up over the prospect of seeing New York play New York? (Especially when New York has already played New York repeatedly during the regular season, under the auspices of interleague competition?)

The indifference was palpable, and it stretched from coast to coast. This is not a nation that despises New York; if it did, the ratings would have soared. This is a nation that, not long ago, became so jaded to the concept of place that even live pictures of men walking on the moon were soon enough shrugged off as routine. No big thing. When the moon becomes a suburb, what does it take to move the people of planet Earth?

Not a few baseball games in close-at-hand boroughs.

Where in the world do you want to go today?

Evidently not Shea Stadium.

––––––––

BOB GREENE is a syndicated columnist for the *Chicago Tribune* and the author of twenty books, including the current national bestseller *Duty: A Father, His Son, and the Man Who Won the War.* The paperback edition of his newest collection of journalism, *Chevrolet Summers, Dairy Queen Nights,* will be published in the spring of 2001.

––––––––

WAKE ME WHEN IT'S OVER

Susan Perabo

In his *Time* magazine column about the Subway Series, New Yorker Joel Stein made the claim that only Yankee fans rooted for the Yankees while "the rest of America" pulled for the Mets. Yet again, the rest of America is profoundly misunderstood by a New Yorker. Fact is, most of us weren't rooting for the Mets. Fact is, most of us weren't rooting for *anyone*.

Nineteen million people (roughly the population of New York State, incidentally) watched Game 2 of the Series. That same Sunday night, at the same time, twenty million of us were watching another New York show, pulling for the guy sitting across from Regis on *Who Wants to Be a Millionaire?*

Stein had one thing right: unless you're a die-hard Yankee fan, it's virtually impossible to root for the Yankees in the World Series, no matter who they're playing. Dynasties are excruciatingly dull when it's not your team making history. Three in a row, four out of five . . . enough already! As a baseball fan, I can appreciate Mariano Rivera's dominance, but that doesn't mean I have to like it. Was it just me, or did even the Yankees themselves seem slightly bored with the whole affair, lazing about on the bench as if it were the second game of a June doubleheader? Where were the crouchers on the dugout steps, the nervous spitters, the bat clutchers?

Oh, wait . . . there they are, in the other dugout. Yes, it's true: the Mets crouched, the Mets spat, the Mets clutched. And there were other things, many things, to like about the Mets' enthusiasm and intensity: Fonzie deftly prowling the middle of the infield, John Franco's genuine ebullience over his first World Series, workhorse Al Leiter hurling his hundred and fortieth pitch of the night, the stupendous grit of those underpaid outfielders. So why not root for the Mets? Why not—in true midwestern spirit—get behind the underdog? Here's why: the Mets don't actually count as an underdog, not to us. The Oakland A's . . . underdog. The Seattle Mariners . . . underdog. We could pull for those teams against the Yanks in the playoffs and mean it. We could have pulled for the Cards, the Giants, even the Braves in a series against the Dynasty. But not the Mets, oh no. Unfair though it may be, for most of the country the Mets are just another team from New York, the precocious little brother of the smugly brilliant Yankees. This sibling rivalry, a decidedly family affair, is what made the Subway Series so much fun for New York, and so little fun for the rest of us. More than ever before, there was nothing remotely World about the World Series.

There are other factors. We all know, for instance, that the Mets are rich. Sure, there's Jay Payton (perhaps the only player in the major leagues who makes less than I do), but overall the Mets' player payroll is third highest in the majors. We like our underdogs poor, or at least middle class. To those of us who suffer through seasons with financially challenged teams like the Royals and Twins, watching rich guys slug it out for the big prize is about as exciting as watching Donald Trump nail the $500,000 question on *Millionaire*.

Then there's the media, who do everything in their power to exacerbate the inferiority complex we may already feel as non–New Yorkers. In all fairness, you New Yorkers probably don't understand the deluge of media attention that your hometown teams get outside New York. Imagine if you moved from New York(!) to a small town in Pennsylvania or Wyoming or New Mexico, picked up the sports section of your local paper, and found on the front page an exhaustingly thorough account of, say, the Houston Astros, and then had to scour page 5 just to find out what your team did last night. When a town anywhere in America has no defined affiliation, the assumption seems to be that by default we'll naturally be interested in the Yankees or the Mets. Ted Turner has worked very hard and has spent about a jillion dollars to make his Atlanta Braves "America's Team." All the Mets and Yankees had to do was be themselves.

Lest you think I'm merely whining, soured by the whole ordeal only because my beloved Cardinals died an ugly death in the NLCS, here's a brief illustration. During the Cardinals/Mets debacle, I spoke to my sister, who lives in Connecticut. She's not much of a baseball fan, but she watched a few innings of the NLCS in order to have something to discuss with the rest of the family for the month of October. During our conversation she made a comment about the New York broadcasters who were doing the television play-by-play in her area.

"There are no New York broadcasters," I told her. "You watch the game on Fox, nationally televised, like everyone else."

"Oh no," she said. "I'm pretty sure I'm picking up a New York station."

"Why?" I asked.

"Because they only talk about the Mets," she said.

Aha! My suspicions confirmed! I had been thinking the same thing all week, but—fearful of being deemed bitter and paranoid by my New York friends— had kept mum about this and chalked up my perceptions to sour grapes. But it's true: player profiles, witty anecdotes, obscure statistics, sentimental stories of past triumphs—80 percent of them focus on the New York team. Even the play-by-play is tainted by New

York bias. When Mike Piazza hits a home run, the commentators howl, "Whoo-hoo . . . he really got a hold of that one!" When Jim Edmonds hits a home run they say, "Ouch . . . that high fastball was Hampton's first mistake of the night!"

Sour grapes? Inferiority complex? In part, perhaps. Sure, I'd have rather seen a Cardinals/Yankees series, a far more historically significant baseball event for true fans across the country than any old Subway Series. But even when my Cardinals lose, I manage without much trouble to find another team to root for in October, an underdog to get behind, players relatively unknown to me to love and support. I mean no disrespect to the Mets or Yankees, nor to their undeniably great fans; I'm only asking for understanding when I admit that, try as I might (and I did try!), I just couldn't muster any authentic excitement about this World Series. I admired individual performances. I enjoyed a few great plays. But I never really *felt* anything. For the first time in my personal World Series history, I changed the channel. Left cold and indifferent by New York/New York, I resigned myself to rooting for the guy in the hot seat.

SUSAN PERABO, a native St. Louisan, teaches creative writing at Dickinson College in Carlisle, Pennsylvania. Her books include the short-story collection *Who I Was Supposed to Be* and an upcoming novel, *The Broken Places*.

HUB FAN BIDS PAIN ADIEU

CHARLES MCGRATH

THERE ARE MORE RED SOX FANS than you might think in New York—Beantown exiles, most of us, but also some, like my son, Ben, who have acquired the affliction through heredity—and for us the Subway Series posed a moral dilemma of almost Sophoclean complexity. Whom to root for?

The alternatives were equally unthinkable. On the one hand, there was the Yankees. The *Yankees!* In this age of free-agentry and expansion teams, it may be hard for younger fans to understand the depth and longevity of the rivalry we Bostonians share with the Yanks, who in 1919 snatched Babe Ruth from us and have then gone on to amass twenty-six World Series titles while we have garnered precisely none. The shame and indignity and heartbreak we have suffered at the hands of the Bronxians is beyond measure or description, but let's start, just as an instance, with the terrible 1978 season.

That was the year when, having shot with unaccustomed swiftness to a comfortable, double-digit lead in the standings, we then squandered it all in a long August and September swoon. I remember listening, at the end of August, to some excruciating games on the West Coast with Ben, who was just a year old. It was then, I think, that he learned the proper carriage of a Red Sox fan—the crossed fingers, the slumped shoulders, the head in the hands. At the end of the season we were tied with guess who, and the pennant was settled with a one-game playoff up at Fenway. We lost of course—on a bloop home run by Bucky Dent, a lazy fly ball that somehow caught a thermal updraft and wafted mercilessly over the left-field wall. "They killed our fathers," one Red Sox fan was heard to say, "and now the sons of bitches are coming after us."

Or how about last year's American League Championship Series? We were the wild card, the Yankees were a year removed from winning the most games ever in a season-plus-postseason. After two nail-biting losses, we beat Clemens in Game 3—or, rather, Pedro did—but then we threw away the fourth game, and in the fifth the wheels all came off: no hitting, no pitching, and certainly no help from the umps, who botched several calls. I e-mailed Ben the next day: "There *is* a God, and he's a prick."

How could I root for a team that had caused me and others such sorrow? And there was also the memory of my poor departed mother to consider. It was she, not my father, who was the baseball fan in our house; while listening to the Sox on the radio, she would nervously smoke her way through an entire pack of Old Golds. When I moved to New York in 1972, she looked me in the eye and said, "I want you to promise me one thing—that you'll never become a Yankee fan."

On the other hand, there was the Mets. The *Mets!* This is the team responsible for the single most painful episode in all of Red Sox history. I'm referring, of course, to the 1986 World Series and in particular to Game 6, when, with the Sox just one strike away from a World Championship (their first since 1918), Mookie Wilson's ground ball dribbled between the croquet-wicket legs of the crippled Bill Buckner, dashing, yet again, the hopes of the Boston faithful. Once we lost that game, it was a foregone conclusion we would lose the next; a rainout the next day only postponed the inevitable, and was a suitable metaphor for the now sodden Red Sox morale. Actually, the Mets weren't solely responsible for this tragedy. I sometimes worry that I may have had something to do with it, for in the top of the tenth, the Championship, in my mind, already secure, I instructed Ben to assemble some spare toilet-paper rolls, so that we could garland the trees of our Mets-loving neighbors. I cringe now at the thought that the same heartless deity who so favors the Yankees might have willed that grounder through just to punish my overweening.

The pain of that game, in any case, is still too

recent, the wound too raw, to be easily forgiven or forgotten, and to make matters worse, the original perpetrator is still part of the Mets organization: Mookie himself, who now coaches first. There he is at every game, a living reminder, standing just a few feet away from where history was made and our fate was sealed. (Coincidentally, another '86 Met, the glowering Lee Mazzilli, holds the equivalent job with the Yankees.)

Yet there is still something a little hapless about the Mets—something almost Red Soxian about their own checkered past. Their team colors are dreadful, and their ballpark is a dump. They have suffered at the hands of the Braves many of the same injustices that we have with the Bombers (and, cruelly, the Braves this year dropped out before the Mets had a chance to exact revenge). In short, the Metsies are lovable in a way that the Yankees can never be, and it was this that, after a night of weighing my heavy options, tipped the balance in my soul. I embraced the Mets as fellow victims—*mes semblables, mes frères!* And then of course I got my heart broken all over again, as the Yankees added yet another jewel to their crown, one that is by now almost comically festooned with glittering gemstones.

Except that this time it didn't feel quite so bad. Maybe pain gets easier to bear the more you have of it, or maybe it's that, in truth, this year's Yankees were a lot less Yankee-like. They stumbled into the Series instead of marching, and until the end their victory was never certain. There were so many question marks in the bullpen, so many cold bats in the dugout, that they reminded me at times of a certain team from New England. When Clemens flung the lumber at Piazza, that was a Yankee thing to do (and it may have signaled, indelibly, his transformation from Bosox to pinstripes). But when Cone came in and, his face etched with anxiety, got Piazza out, I thought of the Red Sox and of the gritty, hard-luck Calvin Schiraldi. Remember him, poor guy? And Sojo's Series-winning hit—it wasn't a lordly Reggie Jackson–like bomb, it was just a little bingle up the middle, the kind of miraculous, seeing-eye hit that the Sox have so often yearned for, and so often failed to get.

———

CHARLES MCGRATH is the editor of *The New York Times Book Review* and frequently writes about sports for *The New York Times Magazine* and other publications.

———

Brooklyn-born John Franco exults at retiring the Yankees in the eighth inning of Game 3; the win came in Franco's first World Series after seventeen years in the big leagues. (*AP Photo/Mark Lennihan*)

GAME 3:
EN LA SERIE MUNDIAL

MARCOS BRETÓN

ORLANDO "EL DUQUE" HERNANDEZ. Pitching. Game
3. World Series. Subway Series. At Shea Stadium.

Diablo!

What a moment.

Qué momento!

Yet it's just before game time and all anyone is
talking about is Roger Clemens hurling a busted bat at
Mike Piazza.

People talk about it in Spanish too, but in español
the whole thing is more a novelty, a side show to the
real show—the right-hander who was a Yankee but
not a Yanqui, a Cuban without a country, a traitor to a
revolution, a symbol of freedom, a rich man whose
money can't buy a homeland.

A busted bat that hits no one?

Americanos. They are so funny.

Por qué? Because there are a lot of people who wish
El Duque was dead, who, if they ever sent something

shooting his way, it sure wouldn't be a piece of wood. And they sure wouldn't miss.

You think Fidel would let El Duque's people watch the game en la isla de Cuba? In Cuba—the cradle of baseball in Latin America? *La cuna de beisbol en Latino America?*

Not in a million years. To the believers, the communists, El Duque is a *gusano*—a worm. He was the coward who sold his soul to the American devil, the American dollar, and then left by the sea—a raft? a sailboat? it doesn't really matter now.

All that matters is that El Duque left—not only his country, but to play baseball for the enemy.

What could be worse for Fidel? Baseball for him, for his Cuba, was the ultimate weapon, the one place where Cubanos and their revolution could whip the Americans at their own game.

When El Duque was on the Cuban National Team, no squad of American college kids could deal with his hook, or with the best players never to reach the big leagues in the last half century.

What a treasure for Fidel: all those wins, those world championships, those Olympic gold medals for *La Revolucíon.* All those photo ops of Fidel, wearing the national team hat with those ridiculous green fatigues.

Think it didn't mean anything to America? In the annual human flood of immigration—the Laotian refugees, the Russians fleeing religious persecution, the starving Mexicans, and the college-educated Indians—who was the one sure bet to be granted residency? The Cuban baseball player.

If you can play, America wants you because it will damn well hurt Fidel.

And so now here was El Duque, in Queens, on the mound. One man dead to the regime of Cuba, but a hero in Miami—where the aging Bay of Pigs refugees live alongside the survivors of the Mariel boat lift, the musician friends of Gloria Estéfan, and the relatives of Elián González.

These were not the fans who fit the uninterested demographic shoved down all our throats—all those people outside New York who didn't care about the Subway Series.

How do you measure ratings anyway?

How do you measure the hatred that every El Duque strikeout triggered in his former country—or the love and admiration they spawned in his new one?

Diablo! In the sixth inning, when there were no outs, three Mets on base, and thousands shouting for blood at Shea—could Fidel ever think that El Duque would give in?

Jay Payton. Slider. Strike three.

Mike Bordick. Fastball. Strike three.

Darryl Hamilton, grounding out on a fielder's choice.

El Duque ran back to the dugout and baseball's Spanish-speaking world could breathe again. At World

Series time, it isn't just Miami's Cubanos behind El Duque. They are with him in Santo Domingo and in Ponce, Puerto Rico; in Maracaibo, Venezuela, and Monterrey, Mexico; and in the Canal Zone de Panama.

And in the Dominican streets around Yankee Stadium, in Boston, New Jersey, Chicago, Denver, Houston, San Francisco, Tijuana. *Diablo!* They were with him every place they speak Spanish and love baseball.

A lot of teams are still clueless as to how to get these people to the ballparks, but they are out there—and for them, every series is a Subway Series.

In 1997, the last time the Yankees didn't win the World Series, the Florida Marlins took it all—led by El Duque's brother, Livan, who was the World Series MVP. His Colombian teammate Edgar Renteria drove home the winning run in Game 7. Their Dominican teammate, Moises Alou, was a singular star. Meanwhile, in the opposing dugout, Sandy Alomar Jr. of Puerto Rico would have been the MVP had his Cleveland Indians not lost in the most excruciating of ways. Omar Vizquel, the Indians' spectacular shortstop, is so popular in his native Venezuela that his country came to a standstill that fall as the Indians marched toward Game 7. Even with President Bill Clinton making his first trip to South America, and Caracas the first stop on a weeklong tour, his visit was secondary news to the great Omar, playing en la Serie Mundial.

This kind of thing happens every year en Latino America.

Por qué?

Because baseball is the Latin game now; they own it. Where El Duque is from, in Cuba, the game took root in the late nineteenth century and spread across the Caribbean basin, linking those countries with a common language and this new secular religion.

Since then, Cuba has been an integral part of American baseball history. Long before Jackie Robinson broke the major league color barrier in 1947, there were Cuban players in the bigs—more than forty of them. They were here before World War I, many of them playing in our nation's capital for the Washington Senators. How were they received? *Diablo!* Americans practiced on them the hatred they would later unleash on Jackie.

But you can't stop progress.

And those great black American players who never got Jackie's chance? They were heroes in Cuba, where the fans cheered Satchel Paige the way Latinos all over Latin America followed the Subway Series in 2000.

Today, the highest paid players in the game are Alex Rodriguez, he of Dominican blood, Carlos Delgado of Puerto Rico, and Manny Ramirez, representing both Santo Domingo and the communidad Dominicana de Washington Heights.

The best starting pitcher? Pedro Martinez of the Dominican Republic.

Baseball's international ambassador? Sammy Sosa, of San Pedro de Macorís, the Dominican Republic.

The game's best reliever? El Duque's teammate, Mariano Rivera of Panama.

And El Duque? All he does is own the postseason.

Even *The New York Times* wrote during the Subway Series that El Duque "has been to baseball what Joe Montana was to the Super Bowl, or what Bill Russell was to the National Basketball Association playoffs. When he pitched, the Yankees won, every time." He was 8–0 in the postseason going into Game 3. No one had ever done that.

In the seventh inning of Game 3, it was still tied: Mets 2, Yankees 2. El Duque had been sick before the game, but he wanted to pitch. His arm felt like it would fall off after the seventh, but he wanted to pitch. Joe Torre wanted to take him out then, but El Duque pleaded his case to stay in. In moments like these, Torre trusted no one more.

El Duque went out for the eighth and struck out his twelfth batter of the game, then gave up a weak single to Todd Zeile. And then Benny Agbayani ended the greatest pitching streak in postseason history with a double. El Duque lost and so did the Yankees, 4–2.

Somewhere, Fidel was feeling like a Mets fan. So were all those communists who wished El Duque were dead. But there would be no sorrow for this Cuban defector. And none for baseball fans throughout Latin America.

That's because you can't stop progress.

Tomorrow, baseball will still be the Latin game.

While El Duque may have lost, the save for the Mets was recorded by Armando Benitez, Dominican.

And tomorrow, the Yankees would win again— Game 4 and then the world championship. Piling all over each other, along with Jeter, O'Neill, and Clemens, were Sojo, Vizcaino, Posada, Martinez, Bernie Williams, and yes, El Duque.

Just weeks before, without El Duque, the Cuban National Team had lost to the Americans in the gold medal game at the Olympics in Sydney. And now this!

Diablo!

Qué momento!

MARCOS BRETÓN is the author of *Away Games: The Life and Times of a Latin Ballplayer,* and collaborated with Sammy Sosa on *Sosa: An Autobiography.* He is a senior writer with the *Sacramento Bee.*

DR. KHAKOO'S TICKET

JIM DWYER

FOR ONE SWEET INSTANT, only the Mets baseball cap on his head kept Dr. Joseph Khakoo's white hair from sailing clear into orbit over Shea Stadium.

As much as anyone around that bawling, joyful asylum in Queens—as much as the Jews for Jesus, the Democrats for Lazio, the drag queens dolled up in Day-Glo orange wigs and royal blue boa feathers, the politicians with girlfriends in one luxury box and wives in another, the fat cats with entourages, the connected and disconnected, the purely mad and the truly devoted—Joe Khakoo had come to cheer.

And a long way he had come, too.

To sit behind him in Loge Box 390 on the night of October 24, 2000, is to hear an American journey, humming across the long-distance wires of memory. On a summer day in 1964, just after Khakoo started as a resident at Roosevelt Hospital, he saw a sign-up sheet posted on a bulletin board. The hospital needed doctors to cover the spectators' first-aid room at Shea Stadium. For a single game, the pay was ten dollars.

"I said, 'Okay, let me take the doubleheader and get fifteen dollars,' " Khakoo would recall.

The assignment came with a pair of field box tickets, not that two seats or twenty mattered much to Khakoo. He couldn't find anyone to come with him. And he didn't know the first thing about baseball. Raised in Zanzibar, a medical student in Bombay, Khakoo in 1964 was new to America and its sports.

"The only thing I heard about the game," he recalled, "was that Marilyn Monroe married a baseball player. Even in Zanzibar, we knew Marilyn Monroe."

Shea Stadium was jammed that summer afternoon in 1964. It turned out that a team from Los Angeles, the Dodgers, was playing at Shea Stadium for the first time, with pitchers named Koufax and Drysdale. Khakoo found the doctors' box and settled in. If any medical emergencies came up, the ushers knew where to fetch him.

"Excuse me, mister, is that seat taken?"

A little boy, eight or nine years old, looked wide-eyed at the empty seat next to Khakoo.

"That's mine, too, but you can sit there," said Khakoo. "Would you like that?"

"Yes, please," said the boy.

The boy cheered when the Mets put the ball in play. He groaned when Koufax broke a killer curve. The doctor, unmoved by the disappointments or small triumphs, sat quietly. The kid quickly realized that the benefactor of his beautiful seat did not know which end was up.

"The batter gets three swings to hit the ball," said the boy. "Koufax is very hard to hit."

"I see," said Khakoo.

"If the players in the field catch the ball before it hits the ground, the batter's out," said the little tutor.

"Where is that one going, he didn't hit the ball?" asked Khakoo.

"Four balls, you walk," said the boy. Three strikes and you're out. Three outs, you're done.

Fortunately, no one needed medical attention as the little boy gave Dr. Khakoo his first lesson in America's sport. By the second game, though, the long afternoon of sun and beer had taken hold of the fans. Dr. Khakoo rallied between the first-aid room and his box seat.

Finally he gave up and stayed with the nurse. By then, he did not want to miss a pitch. Someone arrived with a laceration on his forehead. Khakoo kept an eye on the TV in the medical office.

"That's a fly ball to center fielder!" said Khakoo, delighted to have cracked the code.

No sooner had the man been stitched up than another one arrived with a heart attack. They strapped him to a stretcher, masked him with oxygen, rolled him on his way to the hospital. That Drysdale, he could hurl it, too. And apparently these Los Angeles Dodgers had some past connections to the New York area, through a place in Brooklyn called Ebbets Field. The history explained the hysteria in the stadium.

By the end of the doubleheader, Khakoo was hopelessly hooked on baseball, as played and practiced by its worst team. He covered the first-aid room again a few weeks later, but the Mets' season, of course, ended in September. The next year, he caught another game as the first-aid doc, but his residency at Roosevelt finished in June. He watched. He read. He rooted.

The arc of his life would send him back to Africa for two years, so he was an ocean away when the Miracle Mets of 1969 won the World Series. "Thank goodness someone sent me cuttings from the *Daily News*," he said.

Back in America, he would travel to Cooperstown to see Tom Seaver inducted into the Hall of Fame. Along the way, he became an American citizen. He met and married. His wife and three children love the game.

"All are Mets fans—well, one boy leans slightly toward the Yankees," said Khakoo. "Due to brainwashing by a counselor at summer camp, I believe."

Now he practices pediatric medicine at Harlem Hospital, specializing in hematology, caring for children with sickle-cell anemia. His passion for the Mets is known on every hallway in the hospital. His boss at Harlem, Dr. Steve Nicholas, came up with a few tickets for the Series. So with two out in the ninth inning, as Tuesday the twenty-fourth of October ticked into Wednesday the twenty-fifth, the doctor was in the ballpark to see his first World Series game.

The count climbed to three balls, two strikes. Armando Benitez against the great David Justice. Then, in the span of a blink, Benitez hurled his fastball, Justice's bat knifed through his classic swing, and the ball rose into the October night. A weak popup toward second base. The doctor may have gotten older and wiser in thirty-six years, his hair whiter and wispier, but the very first lesson drilled into his bones at that very first game had not changed: a ball caught on the fly is an out.

And here was Dr. Joseph Khakoo, who learned both the national anthem and national pastime at Shea Stadium, bouncing on air, his curled fists pumping the sky, woofing along to "Who Let the Dogs Out?"

———————

Jim Dwyer, a newspaper writer in New York City, is the author most recently of *Actual Innocence: Five Days to Execution and Other Dispatches from the Wrongly Convicted* (with Peter Neufeld and Barry Scheck). He walks home from Yankee Stadium.

———————

KIDS

ROBERT SULLIVAN

"HEY, DAD," HE SAYS—or just about shouts, actually. He's nine and he's out on the sidewalk, out in the stream of early morning schoolgoers, blocking the traffic of men and women on their way to work all uniformed in suits and geared up with phones.

"Dad!" he says again.

I'm drawing my last desperate sip of coffee, forcing the cup down to the table as I do. I am checking my pockets for keys and change, as if indiscreetly signaling some third-base coach no one can see.

He's getting impatient now, wondering what's taking me so long, naturally oblivious to the fact that it took me half an hour to convince him to put on his shoes and socks. "Dad!" he says. *"Dad!"* he repeats, more urgently this time. "Who's *this?*"

He bats lefty, though he is not a lefty, though there is no actual bat. His right leg is up, his right toe pointed like the toe of a ballerina, a considered grace. His practice swing is slow, level, smooth, measured, with one eye closed, one eye opened—the open eye regarding all in a self-style check, a measuring up. Practice swing one. At this point, I'm locking the door. Practice swing two. I'm turning around now, wondering if I forgot his schoolbag again. Practice swing three. I notice that he's just nearly swatted some guy with a briefcase who's fielding a call from the office.

And before I can find my coat, before I can get out the front door, the invisible pitch has arrived, so that this veteran nine-year-old imaginary pro winds up, lifts the right leg, makes a little kick, leans back, and then—*Bam!*—the imaginary ball is going, going, out of the park, out of sight, in his mind. He watches the ball fade away. There's a pause of sufficiently realistic duration while the imaginary crowd roars. He raises his hand coolly toward the stoop.

"Who was *that?*" he says, beaming. Never mind—he can't *wait* for the answer. "Dad, it was *O'Neill!*"

And so it went, during the Subway Series, in the days before, in the days during, and even now, as basketball season fails to catch on in the same way, as football pales in comparison and hockey is barely on the radar screen. Not that we didn't spend the entire summer pantomiming O'Neill and Justice, Posada and Jeter—the ritual repeated throughout the day, at school pick-up time, during the execution of homework, at dinner. The city had a low-grade fever—I watched an entire subway car discuss (politely or even civilly) the Subway Series one afternoon—but the kids had the Series bad. I remember, for example, the corner of DeGraw and Court Streets, on a summer night, near the plastic chairs outside Sal's Pizza, the greasy slices left untouched. Three boys were wowing each other with the nuances of their favorite pitchers, blazing in imaginary fastballs, following up with unbelievable sliders, change-ups, curves, every pitch a perfect strike.

"Clemens!" the one guy shouts.

"Right!" the other guy says.

"Okay," says the third guy, raising up his knee way, way up into the air.

He is stopped mid-pitch. "El Duque!" the shorter one says.

There's a collective shrug, as if you'd have to be an alien not to know that, as if the identity of the pitcher had never been a question in this case, in the case of El Duque.

Now the pizza-stained hand rises again, and the catcher's signal—coming, evidently, from somewhere near the trash can on the corner—gets a nod. The pitch is perfect, theoretically pure, a Platonic form of a pitch that can be seen only by the philosopher kings of the world, who in this particular New York City polity are in third and fourth grade. Two simultaneous top-of-the-lungs shouts rise up in the almost-bedtime air: *"Rivera!"*

Like most New Yorkers, our imaginary star did not attend any of the Subway Series games. But the Series changed our daily life. At the pastry shop, he stood with his little sister in the Yankee line at the counter and tried desperately not to smile at the guy who would serve only fans of the Mets. He fielded calls nightly from aunts and uncles and grandparents. And God knows what was going on in school.

"Does anybody want the Yankees?" I asked at one point.

"No, Dad. Pretty much everybody likes the Mets."

(Demographic note: The Mets rule in our neighborhood.)

"*Nobody* likes the Yankees?"

"Well, there are two guys who kind of don't care whether the Yankees or the Mets win . . ."

"What about the girls?"

He rolls his eyes. "The girls like Derek Jeter, Dad."

We did attend two pennant games, and if there is a heaven, it is a place where fathers get to sit next to their sons during home runs by Bernie Williams. The game against Seattle that we saw was a nail-biter: one long will-they-do-it, come-from-behind game with one, then two, then seven runs, so that finally the boy is cheering, shouting, happy-ing himself hoarse. Then he turned his eyes away from the field for just one moment, just long enough for his dad to see a pure un-homeworked, bottomless joy—a perfect-game bliss that dissolves into a long, frantic, unselfconscious bear-cub hug.

When the Series finally happened, it was mostly during a school week, and the games went way, way past bedtime. Still, he was chased off to bed only when he began to exhibit the first signs of sleep deprivation, which is to say around the fourth or fifth inning. There is no doubt his math homework took a hit, and maybe his knowledge of African geography will always suffer some because of Game 5. But it was the Subway Series, after all, and he scored high in my book when I recently hit him with a pop Subway Series quiz:

Q: In the last game, when the Yankees won it, when did you finally fall asleep?

A: When I saw Rivera come in, because then I knew everything was going to be, you know, okay.

Q: What was the last thing you remember about the last game?

A: I remember trying not to fall asleep.

These days, he's getting to bed earlier and catching up on his sleep and I am, if I may say so, getting better at his game.

"Dad, who's *this*?" he says. The bat held high, gyroscoped slowly, tauntingly, until the pitch, and then the big elegant swing.

"Justice?"

"No, Jeter!" His head shakes, exasperatedly. "Okay, who's this?"

Pause, concentration. "Bernie Williams."

Big smile, high five. *Right!*

———

ROBERT SULLIVAN is the author of *The Meadowland* (Anchor) and *A Whale Hunt* (Scribner). He lives in Brooklyn, New York, with his wife and two children.

———

Notice served: Derek Jeter watches his first-pitch leadoff home run give the Yankees a lead they would not relinquish in the pivotal Game 4. (*AP Photo/Charles Krupa*)

GAME 4:
LEGACY

PETER KNOBLER

I WAS A HUGE GIANTS FAN. Born and raised in Manhattan. And in 1954, when I was seven years old—the first year I collected baseball cards, the first year I knew anything about or can even remember baseball—not only did the Giants win the pennant, they won the World Series. Forty-six years later, I can name those Giants starters the way some people can name saints. I thought my team was supposed to win every year. Who knew it would never happen again?

My son, Daniel, is eleven. Born and raised in Manhattan. Daniel is genetically hard-wired into the Subway Series. His mother, my wife, Jane, was born on the day Bobby Thomson hit the Polo Grounds "Shot Heard 'Round the World" that demolished the Dodgers and put the Giants into the Series against the Yankees. (Her father is one of the rare New Yorkers of a certain age who swears he was *not* at that game. We're not so sure.)

Daniel was seven in 1996 when the Yankees won the World Series. We were there, in the upper deck of Yankee Stadium, way down the left-field line, Daniel standing on the seat next to me so we were at eye level, my arm around his waist as Mark Lemke's pop foul settled into Charlie Hayes's glove and the place went nuts. The difference is, my son's team keeps winning. Daniel is the Derek Jeter of Yankee fans; he thinks this happens every year. And so far he's pretty much been right.

The day before a kid's memory kicks in could be another millennium. So even though the Yankees had won five straight World Series from 1949 through '53, four out of five of which had been Subway Series, I didn't know anything about them; they belonged to someone else. The '55 Series was mine. My father appeared in the door of my fourth-grade classroom like a manager calling a prospect up to the majors, pulled me out of school, and took me to Game 1.

These are things you don't forget. It was a bright, crisp day, blue sky, late September yellow sun, World Series weather. We took the Lexington Avenue IRT to the Bronx, walked on River Avenue behind the center-field bleachers, browsed past the souvenir stands with facsimile team-autographed baseballs and stand-up cards full of color-photograph buttons, about the size of a quarter, of each Yankee player—Scooter, Mickey, Gil McDougald, Irv Noren. The cards were emptying fast but there were a lot of Norens left. My pop asked me what I wanted and I settled on a packet of eight-by-ten glossies of everyone on the team. We passed through the gate and I held my father's hand as we walked up the concrete ramp, and each time I glimpsed the stunningly green field behind the last row of seats or down a cement corridor, I caught my breath.

We were sitting in the loge, near first base. Me to my father's left, closest to home plate. There was a dark vertical I beam a half-dozen seats down the row that supported the upper deck and blocked the view of everyone behind it, but my father and I had no obstruction. Yankees-Dodgers, and I was a Giants fan, I hated the Dodgers. We bought a program and I scored the game.

Don Newcombe started for the Dodgers. When Roy Campanella tossed the ball to third base for Jackie Robinson to rub up, the umpire tossed that ball out and told Newk to rub them up himself. Mickey Mantle was hurt and didn't play. Joe Collins hit two home runs. Jackie Robinson stole home and Yogi Berra stormed around the umpire like a furious jack-in-the-box. The Yankees won, 6–5. Though I could have stayed there forever, we took the D train back to Manhattan. Got home in time for dinner. I remember it like it happened this afternoon.

Fourteen years later I showed up at my father's office with two tickets to Game 3 of the Mets-Orioles

Series and pulled my pop out of work to take him to Shea Stadium. Tommie Agee made two spectacular catches for the Miracle Mets that day. The Mets won. My pop was more than pleased.

So when I scored two tickets to Game 4 of the 2000 World Series, there was no one else I considered taking except my son.

Television commerce stole from me the opportunity to take Daniel out of class. I'd have done it in a heartbeat; there is no history lesson more valuable, no cultural moment more passionately memorable, than a pilgrimage to the Series.

The game was scheduled to start at 8:18 P.M. I suppose we could have driven. Daniel had been falling asleep in front of the television around the eighth inning of the first three games, and I was concerned about dragging my boy through the New York City public transit system at one in the morning on a school night. But this was a Subway Series and it was important to take the subway. We took the No. 9 local to Times Square, walked down two flights of stairs, and caught the No. 7 Flushing express out to Shea.

"This is the train John Rocker made all those moron comments about," I told Daniel.

"I know, Dad," he said. How foolish of me.

The Transit Authority had unveiled new, clean Subway Series cars for the occasion, but we must have missed those; ours were the ones that people actually ride, and they didn't work all that well. The lights kept browning out as we rounded curves and passed between stations. Daniel got worried.

"Think of it as an amusement park ride," I offered.

"I don't like amusement park rides," he said.

The platform at Shea smelled of the fresh coat of paint the TA had slapped on. The crowd was thick. Daniel reached for my hand. We walked behind the bleachers, passed the Major League Baseball merchandise tent, which forty minutes before game time had an hour-long line to get in ("We'll get something after the game, I promise," I said after a five-minute wait), circled the stadium, and took an elevator to our seats.

Press level, near first base. There was a TV monitor near the ceiling four seats down from us so we could catch replays if we missed anything. Daniel sat to my left, closest to home plate. His eyes about bugged out. Under the lights the grass was a brilliant green, the infield dirt the color of burnished leather. The Taj Mahal, Versailles, the Summer Palace—there is no more beautiful place in the world than a ballpark before a game. "Oh, Dad!" he said. "This is so cool!"

Daniel spent all nine innings leaning forward against the rail, perched literally on the edge of his seat. I know, I was watching him watch the game. First pitch, Jeter parked one into the left-field bleachers. Daniel's favorite ballplayer, Paul O'Neill, tripled to the right-center-field gap and scored on Scott Brosius's sac fly to center. Jeter tripled his second time up and had a shot at hitting for the cycle. Mike Piazza hit a two-run monster to pull the Mets within a run. It was a one-run game from the third inning on. David Cone came out of the bullpen and oblivion to get Piazza to pop out. O'Neill made a clutch sliding catch of an Edgardo Alfonzo line drive right in front of us. Mariano Rivera pitched two innings of scoreless relief. Daniel will remember these names as if they're all saints. The Yankees won, 3–2.

It took half an hour to buy him a Yankee cap, but we weren't leaving without one. The 7 train, brimming with baseball fans in the afterglow of a great game, wasn't so intimidating on the ride home. It was one-thirty by the time we came through the door. "Dad," Daniel told me, "I don't have words to describe my feelings." He will. He'll tell his son all about it.

PETER KNOBLER collaborated with James Carville and Mary Matalin on *All's Fair: Love, War, and Running for President.* Shortstop for the Seaview All-Stars, he wrote *Giant Steps* with Kareem Abdul-Jabbar and *Living the Dream* with Hakeem Olajuwon. His collaboration with Viacom chairman Sumner Redstone will be published this spring by Simon & Schuster.

A BRONX TALE

MARY HIGGINS CLARK

IT WAS 1949. The Clark home on Narragansett Avenue in the Bronx had always been a mecca for the friends of the three Clark brothers, but this year it was even more special. The Clarks had a newly acquired television set, and for the first time would be seeing the World Series on it. A Subway Series! The Yankees and the Brooklyn Dodgers.

Newly engaged to Warren Clark, I was one of the privileged group who got to sit around the living room eagerly awaiting the opening pitch. The TV was on, and we stared raptly at the ten-inch black-and-white screen showing the station pattern. In those days there were many hours when there was no actual programming scheduled, and only the station pattern was proof that the TV set was working.

The Clarks' housekeeper, L. Johnston, walked through the room, paused, looked at the set, studied the screen, and folded her arms. "My son has one that moves," she said smugly.

During all the clamor and excitement about the potentiality and then the actuality of a Subway Series in this past summer 2000, I found my mind turning back to that first Subway Series. To be perfectly honest, I was then only mildly interested in the game, and far more interested in the engagement ring sparkling on my finger and daydreaming about the Christmas wedding we were planning.

Fast-forward to the present. This year I didn't miss watching a game of either the playoffs or the series. I rooted for both the Mets and the Yankees to win their pennants, but for the Yankees to win the Series. Now if the Mets had won, I could have lived with it. They have a great team and it would have been nice to see them covered with glory. But that generosity of spirit evaporated when the fifth game was ending and our team, our Yankees-of-the-Bronx team, did it again.

"Take me out to the ball game. Take me out with the crowd. Buy me some peanuts and Cracker Jack. I don't care if I ever come back."

If you grew up in the Bronx as I did, that song seemed to float in the air from opening day of the baseball season to the last pitch of the World Series. A summer job at the Stadium was Shangri-la for the high school boys. Many of them earned their tuition to

Fordham Prep or Xavier Academy by selling hot dogs and sodas there while Joltin' Joe DiMaggio made history on the field.

They also earned the money to cover their Saturday-night dates. Looking back, I remember that going to the movies and having a soda at the ice cream parlor were sometimes financed by my date's earnings from the Yankee game that day. And if it had been a particularly good day for hot dog sales, then my date might take me to the Paradise on the Grand Concourse, only a short hop from Yankee Stadium. A ticket to the other theaters cost a dime. The Paradise with its lush ceiling of stars and roomy chairs meant the guy was plunking down a staggering twenty-five cents each.

My interest in baseball grew by osmosis. You can't be married to a dedicated fan and not pick up some of the beat and excitement of the game. In 1949, Warren's Brooklyn Dodgers lost to the Yankees. But two years later a second chance at glory was within their grasp. The Dodgers and the Giants were playing the final game to see who would win the pennant and be in the World Series against the Yankees.

I remember the last 1951 game particularly well. We were living in an apartment in Manhattan. The second baby was on the way. Warren was so positive that the Dodgers would win the pennant that he had bet a week's salary on the outcome. When I heard about that I rooted for the Dodgers to win with the same fervor he was displaying.

The rubber game. The last pitch. I can still see Bobby Thomson on that grainy screen hit the shot heard 'round the world. Bye-bye to a week's salary!

In 1955 Warren's unlimited faith in the Dodgers was justified when in a cliffhanging seventh game they at last won the World Series.

Nine years later, on a warm and beautiful afternoon, a friend who had attended Warren's funeral that morning took me aside. "I have tickets to the Stadium," he said. "It might be a distraction for the kids to see a game." He rounded up the three oldest, piling them in the car with his own son, and they were on the way.

Looking back I realize that baseball games were not only about sportsmanship and fun; they were a comfort zone as well. A reward for the good student, a birthday celebration, a distraction for the grieving.

Now all these years later my ten-year-old grandson, "brokenhearted," as he confided, by not winning a tight election to the leadership group of the student council, was asked what would help him to swallow the bitter pill of defeat. A devoted Yankees fan, he had the answer: "A ticket to the World Series."

Two nights later at Shea Stadium, he was cheering on his Yankees in what is *his* first Subway Series.

In closing, may I offer a tip of the hat to all the boys of summer, the players and managers and coaches, past and present? A thousand thanks for all the plea-sure you've given us over the years.

And may I ask a quick question? Do you think it's greedy to hope that the gods are smiling and we'll be enjoying another Subway Series next year?

Maybe not.

———————

MARY HIGGINS CLARK is the author of twenty-two worldwide best-sellers. She lives with her husband, John Conheeney, in Saddle River, New Jersey.

———————

NEW YORK'S HEROES

DONNA HANOVER

TRUE CONFESSIONS: I didn't know their earned run averages, their career win totals, or their on-base percentages before the Subway Series got under way. I still don't know these or probably a lot of other vital baseball statistics for the Mets or Yankees.

On the other hand, I have had the chance to get to know some of the players and coaches as people; my children and I have had the privilege of riding in four ticker-tape parades honoring the World Series champions; and I've played ball on the field at Yankee Stadium. So while I may not have grown up taking the trolley to Ebbets Field, this year's World Series was still a personal thing for me.

Like so many New Yorkers, I was first drawn to baseball by the talent of Willie Mays. I grew up in the San Francisco Bay area because my father was stationed at naval bases around there; my first baseball memories are of listening to Giants games. Even if you were young and new to the game, you couldn't miss the excitement when Willie stepped up to the plate, or raced to the spot of a fly ball so he could make a basket catch. Also, when visiting my grandfather in southern California, I'd hear Vin Scully describing the Dodgers games through the static of that wonderful modern invention, the transistor radio.

When I moved to New York for the first time, for grad school in journalism at Columbia in the early seventies, there was Willie in center field for the Mets—though, to tell you the truth, I wasn't watching much baseball then. I've never been one of those day-in-day-out fans; I like the excitement of postseason play. The atmosphere of big games is irresistible, and I've been lucky enough to see several of them.

One of the things that's made the Yankees special in their title run is that, like the teams in the older days of baseball, they've kept the team together from year to year. There are changes around the field, of course—a David Justice, a Roger Clemens—but the heart of the team remains the same. For the casual fan, that makes the players feel like a part of the family, the way players used to when we were all a lot younger.

My own family is a bit partisan toward the Yankees, of course. It revolves around my son, who has been in pinstripes pretty much since birth—he came home from the hospital in Yankee pajamas. My daughter came with me to the second game of the Subway

Series; New York baseball is a kid-centered matter for me. I think we're lucky in this city, that so many of the players are also wonderful people; I'm sure they have their wild sides, but so many of them are true gentlemen, and I'm happy as a mother for my kids to have a Tino Martinez or a Derek Jeter to look up to.

There's a special place in my heart for the Torres. I interviewed Joe's wife, Ali, about their battle with Joe's prostate cancer. The article for *Good Housekeeping* magazine was her first public discussion of Joe's medical condition and what it had meant to their marriage. A lovely, tall, confident but soft-spoken woman, Ali told me she first went into denial when the news came that Joe's PSA count was high. He got very quiet—the only sign he gave of being anxious, so much like his demeanor on the bench during tight games. When the diagnosis was confirmed, it was a very emotional time for him. She kicked into survival mode, comforting him and researching their options thoroughly. While Joe napped with their little daughter Andrea upstairs, she described to me their approach with the same words Joe has used in good times and tough times for the Yankees: "We're a team."

I've gotten involved with the Yankees in charitable causes linked to the fight against ALS, Lou Gehrig's disease. The cause is an important one to the team; they've never forgotten that it was in their stadium that Gehrig declared himself to be "the luckiest man on the face of the earth." The Yankees do more than just give their time; they've also hosted some great fund-raisers, including a game between the casts of the soap operas *One Life to Live* and *All My Children*, played at Yankee Stadium. I'll never forget getting up to bat in that game—me, batting in Yankee Stadium! I want to report for all to know that I did get wood on the ball; it was an out, but at least I made contact. What a thrill! When it came time for the real game to start, the Yankees had the actor Michael Zaslow, who was struck down with ALS, throw out the first pitch. He could no longer walk at the time, but he sat in a golf cart, and when the catcher came out to get that ceremonial pitch, Michael motioned him back so he could feel like he was throwing a real pitch in his own field of dreams. It was a beautiful moment in a special place.

The Mets join with the Yankees in a real commitment to the community that supports them so well. I felt affectionate sadness for them at the outcome of the Series; I've broadcast from their bullpen for *Good Day New York,* and have lunched each year with several of the players and coaches at Shea as they honor youngsters chosen by St. Mary's Foundation for Children. Bobby Valentine is my co-presenter at those banquets, and he's always great with the kids. The Mets also spearheaded a drive to get kids to wear protective headgear when they're bicycling or skateboarding: "We wear our helmets," the ads said, "and you should wear yours."

All in all, I don't think we could ask for better representatives of New York than the men who fought so hard for the World Series title in the stadiums of the Bronx and Queens this fall. On and off the field, they do everything anyone could ask to live up to the spotlight that comes with their real job: being not just athletes, but heroes.

―――――――

DONNA HANOVER is a journalist, actress, and the First Lady of the City of New York.

―――――――

THE GOODEST GUYS

DAVID REMNICK

SOME TIME AFTER MIDNIGHT, Joe Torre walked slowly into a low-slung media room in the bowels of Shea Stadium carrying a flute of champagne. He held his glass with pinkie-out panache, as if he had trained all his life for a role in *Design for Living*, but his face registered nothing like serenity or elation. His jowls slumped, his eyes were funereal, red-rimmed. He'd been crying for a while now, unashamed, burying his face in the crook of his arm, hugging his wife, his players, even George Steinbrenner (what a man must do!). Now he eased into his chair with an exhausted old-guy sigh. It was as if this victory—leading the Yankees to their third straight World Series title, the first team to three-peat since the Oakland A's did it twenty-six years ago—were merely a relief, the relief of not failing.

Where was the crowing? Where was the joy? Even now, flanked by Andy Pettitte, who had pitched the night through with such intelligence and gall, and Luis Sojo, the lumpy role player who'd whacked home the winning runs off Al Leiter in the top of the ninth, Torre focused most keenly not on the highlights, the big hits, but rather on the game's slender margins. His hair slick with Mumm's and Bud, the shampoo of champions, he sensed the abyss. With two out in the bottom of the ninth, the Yanks leading 4–2, and a man on base for the Mets, Mike Piazza had cracked one to center field off the most indomitable man on the Yankee payroll, Mariano Rivera.

"I screamed, 'No!'" Torre said. "It was probably the most scared I've been."

Only when Bernie Williams trotted back nearly to the warning track, looked up into the cool hazy night for the ball, and found it spinning into his glove for the last out—only then could Torre afford to think something other than the worst.

"Any time Piazza hits a ball in the air, it's a home run in my mind," he said.

It was infinitely worse, of course, down the hall. One after another—Piazza, Leiter, Benny, Fonzie—the Mets tromped heavily through Shea's tunnels. They had that vacant, battle-weary stare you see in First World War prints. They didn't speak, didn't acknowledge their wives, their heartbroken kids. Their steel spikes clicked on the concrete floor.

Bobby Valentine, the Mets manager, answered for them all, but he blamed only himself. He'd left his pitcher in too long. Leiter, like all true starters, had promised his manager everlasting endurance, and so Valentine followed his heart and not the cold logic of the scorecard. "I was wrong," Valentine said. "It was the wrong decision, obviously. If I'd brought somebody else in, they definitely would have gotten the guy out, and we'd still be playing." And then he walked off and hugged the Mets co-owner, Fred Wilpon, hugged him hard, a terrible embrace.

They're amazing, these scenes. No one's died, everyone's rich, it's a kid's game, and yet . . . For a few minutes, for the cameras, partly out of joy, partly from a sense of ritual, the winners douse each other with champagne. They drench the mayor, toast the owner. But it breaks up pretty quickly, and even some of the players, most of them not yet as careworn as Torre, look strung out, overtired, impatient to go home. It was as if they were beginning to realize that the smell coming up from the locker-room rug was worse than a frat house on a Sunday morning. Enough. "Can't a guy get a shower around here?" Derek Jeter said. It was time to go get lost.

Roger Clemens tore back the plastic sheeting that covered his locker, grabbed his pants, and said to no one in particular, "This champagne is burning my eyes." And that was pretty much all he'd said in days.

Like it or not, the lasting image of this World Series will undoubtedly be that of Clemens winging that broken bat back at Piazza in the first inning of Game 2.

Aesthetes and true fans everywhere will prefer to talk into the night about the more elevated moments: how two of the most brilliant pitching performances of the Series—El Duque's in Game 3 and Leiter's in Game 5—were, in fact, defeats; we'll look to Paul O'Neill's triples and masterfully long at-bats, to his helmet-slamming moments of frustration even as he hit for a Series average of .474. But the broken-bat tape is forever. Baseball's Zapruder film, some of the TV guys called it. The next morning, Don Imus was on WFAN joking about the "second-bat theory" and some columnists were talking in terms of a psychotic episode. In the *News*, Mike Lupica referred to Clemens and his "Mike Tyson moment." Some beat writers and columnists for the dailies even felt that Piazza and the Mets had betrayed the imperatives of retribution and machismo in failing to rush the mound and pummel the pulp out of Clemens. "Meek the Mets" was the headline over Wallace Matthews's attack in the *Post*.

The sanest reaction, I thought, came from Piazza himself. For World Series week, Piazza had agreed to an old tabloid tradition. He would "write" a daily column for the *Post*; that is, he would let the paper run his postgame quotes in the form of a bylined article. He was angry, but mainly he was bewildered by the "bizarre" incident; most of all, he resented that the press was asking him why he had not gone after Clemens. Grow up, Piazza counseled the hysterics: "The situation happened. It's done. Argue it left and right. Okay, should I go out and bleeping kill the guy? It's the World bleeping Series and I get suspended, now I can't bleeping play in the World Series. So I go out and kill the guy, I'm bleeping selfish and I look like a hero to some guys. Meanwhile we go out and bleeping lose the World Series 'cause I'm suspended for a couple of games. Anybody else who is not in that position doesn't know what the bleep they're talking about. Sorry about the bleeps. The more I write, the more emotional I get." (Join the bleeping club, Mike.)

"Emotion" was the very word Clemens used to describe his (a) confusion, (b) transgression, (c) regression, (d) all of the above. Ever since Clemens beaned Piazza in July, the great tabloid narrative had been building to this confrontation. He was in a frazzle prior to the game and worse when the first inning ended. Before coming out for the second, Clemens was like an overwrought kid giving himself a "timeout": he went off to a special room to be alone and settle down.

Clemens is thirty-eight now, and he has been tightly wound for as long as he has been in the majors. Lupica's Tyson analogy—with its hint of gnawed-upon ears—is extreme, but Clemens does gear up for his starts like a fighter. To strengthen his hands, he fills a big bowl with uncooked rice and squeezes handfuls of it. His house is filled with exercise machines. Every time he pitches, he comes close to destroying his arm. His freezer is loaded with bags of ice that he uses to stem the inflammation. When Clemens was pitching for the Red Sox, the team's physical therapist, Rich Zawacki, said, "I've never seen a pitcher whose body breaks down the way his does in a game. . . . Basically, we wind up piecing him back together from game to game." And that was ten years ago. "If someone met me on a game day, he wouldn't like me," Clemens told *Sports Illustrated* back then, and things haven't changed at all. "The days in between, I'm the goodest guy you can find. On the day of a game? If I'm watching television with you, I'm not hearing you, and I'm not hearing the television. . . . I want to be relentless. I want to pound guys. Once you pound guys, everything is quicker. I know how it is. I know how I felt those times when I started out against Nolan Ryan or Tom Seaver or Dwight Gooden. I know how guys feel when they face me now."

The rest of the country, or much of it, according to the TV ratings, thought of the Subway Series as the ball-yard equivalent of the Iran-Iraq war: "A pox on 'em both." "At least, one New York team has to lose." That sort of thing. And, truth be told, there were moments that you didn't necessarily want aired west of the Hudson. It was not a source of great pride, for example, to see the governor, George Pataki, sitting in his box at Game 1 wearing a Yankee sweatshirt and taking as his ballpark refreshment . . . white wine. Nor was there any happy explanation for the way some Yankee fans discovered a rationale for booing Piazza every time he came to bat.

But there were countless true fans, crazed fans, intelligent fans everywhere, all over the city. For Game 5, at Shea, I sat up in the mezzanine near the left-field foul pole. I had on my right a friend who saw his first World Series game in 1941, the Mickey Owen dropped-third-strike game. He had the equanimity of his years, dividing his admiration between O'Neill's twilight struggles and Leiter's march to Waterloo. On my left was a Mets fan, one Joyce Mandelkern of Port Washington, Long Island, whose comments to her husband all night were so quick and insightful, and whose emotions were so raw, that I couldn't resist getting to know her. She told me that when she watched the Mets at home she turned off the sound to keep the tension at a manageable level, and that when things got out of control she'd go to her garage and sit in the car. "Sometimes it's just too unbearable," she said.

The awful moment came Thursday night at 11:42 P.M. Top of the ninth. Yankees up. Men on first and second. Luis Sojo at bat. Al Leiter readied himself on the mound. Joyce Mandelkern of Port Washington buried her face in her arm.

"I can't watch this!" she said.

Then came the pitch.

DAVID REMNICK is the editor of *The New Yorker*. He is also the author of *King of the World* and *Lenin's Tomb*, which won the Pulitzer Prize for nonfiction in 1994.

A stunned Al Leiter watches Luis Sojo's four-hopper bound up the middle for two runs in the ninth inning of the deciding game. *(AP Photo/Bill Kostrou)*

GAME 5:
CHANGING TRAINS

JOHN FEINSTEIN

FOR ME, GOING TO BASEBALL GAMES always meant the subway. It was the No. 1 train to Times Square, then down the steps to the brand-new No. 7 train en route to Shea Stadium, or the No. 1 train to 59th Street, where you could transfer from the IRT to the IND for free and take the D train from there to Yankee Stadium.

I knew every stop on both lines. I knew which car to ride in to make the quickest exit from the platform to the ballpark. It cost $1.30 to sit upstairs at a Mets game, $1.50 to sit upstairs for the Yankees. It was a lot easier to sneak downstairs at Yankee Stadium than at Shea Stadium because fewer kids went to see the Yankees so the ushers weren't as on the alert for us.

All those subway trips, all those hours in the two ballparks, and the thought of a Subway Series never once occurred to me. That was history-book stuff. My father had told me about all the years of frustration in Brooklyn rooting for the Dodgers and I knew all about 1955 and Johnny Podres and how the Dodgers and Giants moving west was the reason the Mets came into being. But a Subway Series? Yankees vs. Mets? No way.

I was a Mets fan, probably because every other kid in the neighborhood was a Yankees fan. The Mets were still awful when I first came to baseball, and the Yankees still champions. I can remember the first time I looked for the standings in a newspaper in 1962. The Yankees were in first place, the Mets were in last with a record of 15–48. For some reason, the Mets record sticks with me. They became my team. I never hated the Yankees, they were just another team to me. What they did never affected the Mets, so I had nothing against them.

My favorite Met in the early days was Al Jackson, whom Bob Murphy always—*always*—called Li'l Al Jackson as if that was his full name. Li'l Al shut out the Cardinals 1–0 on the last Friday night of the 1964 season, and I couldn't understand why winning eight games prevented him from winning the Cy Young Award.

As anyone who has followed baseball for more than fifteen minutes knows, the Mets went from awful to extraordinary in one season. They did *not* go from worst to first; they were ninth in 1968, winning

73 games, a major breakthrough at the time. But then came the Miracle of '69. I went to 66 games at Shea that season, but also squeezed in 25 trips to the Bronx. By then, the Yankees were in their fifth straight season of mediocrity, so the rise of the Mets never once put the words "Subway Series" on anyone's lips.

My love affair with the Mets was severely damaged on the night of June 15, 1977, when Tom Seaver was traded. For the next few seasons, as the team floundered—the Yankees were again winning championships by then—I paid little attention to them. I graduated from college, went to work at *The Washington Post*, and began to see baseball and baseball players more as a working reporter than a wide-eyed kid. Change came gradually rather than all at once.

In 1980, I wrote a lengthy feature story on Seaver. I sat with him in the clubhouse in Houston for several hours one afternoon asking him in detail about the events of 1969. I remembered *everything*, from the West Coast trip in May that turned the season around to his imperfect game in July to the twin 1–0 shutouts of the Pirates in September, in which the starting pitchers (Jerry Koosman and Don Cardwell) drove in the winning run in each game. Seaver's memory wasn't nearly as clear. "Was it the Pirates?" he asked about the doubleheader. Sure it was, I said, September fifth, a Friday twi-nighter. "I thought we got swept in that doubleheader," he said. No, no, I explained, that was two weeks later at Shea. This was in Pittsburgh.

Seaver shrugged. "See, you have all these memories as a fan," he said. "For a player, it's different. Winning that year was great and it was exciting, but it was our job." A job. My hero was telling me baseball was a job for him in 1969. The greatest, most thrilling summer of my life, and it was a *job*?

I survived that trauma and came back to the Mets in 1984 when Dwight Gooden arrived on the scene—a young Seaver, only more talented. The Mets made it back to the World Series in 1986 and I was there as a reporter, though hardly an objective one. When the ball went through Billy Buckner's legs I almost hit my head on the press box ceiling. Then I went to the Red Sox clubhouse because Buckner was my story. I stood there and watched Buckner answer every question, if not once, then fifty times. He never snapped at anyone; never tried to escape; never threw his hands up and said no more, go away. I wrote that night that Buckner was a hero trapped in the role of goat. I still believe that.

The more I've covered sports through the years, the less I've rooted for uniforms and the more I've rooted for people. The day the renowned media-basher Pat Riley became coach of the Knicks was the day I stopped rooting for the Knicks. I've never looked back. In 1995, the Yankees traded for David Cone. That winter Joe Torre became the manager. I had gotten to know both researching a baseball book in 1992. They were two of the most likeable people I had ever met in sports.

Suddenly I found myself watching Yankee games even when the Mets were on. That had never happened before. Then Bobby Valentine took over the Mets late in 1996, and in 1998, for the first time the words started being whispered: Subway Series. The Mets flamed out in September of that season, then came up two games shy of the Series in '99. This fall, it finally happened: Mets vs. Yankees. Subway Series.

I kept telling myself I was rooting for the Mets because rooting for the Mets would mean I was still hanging on to some part of that kid who remembered the details of 1969 more vividly than Tom Seaver did. But when Mike Piazza's last line drive screamed into the night, my heart jumped—with fear. When Bernie Williams settled under the ball, I let out a deep breath. I couldn't fool myself any longer. I admired the Mets because they were a gritty team, a stand-up team, a team that never gave up. They had, as the saying goes in my business, a good clubhouse.

But I wanted the Yankees to win. I wanted Cone's farewell to New York to be on a ride through the Canyon of Heroes. I wanted another title for Torre and the core group he had managed so well for the last five years. I felt guilty for feeling that way. I felt old for feeling that way.

A Subway Series finally happened. But it happened long after I had left the subways behind.

JOHN FEINSTEIN is the author of twelve books, most recently *The Last Amateurs—In Search of Glory and Honor in Division I College Basketball*. He writes columns for America Online and *Golf* magazine and is a commentator for National Public Radio.

ROGER AND HILLARY

TERRY GOLWAY

IT MAY NOT HAVE BEEN A Subway Series for the ages—the five-game Yankee romp was a little too abrupt and one-sided to deserve mention with epics past—but it surely was a Subway Series for the age. Even though the spirits of Jackie Robinson, Mickey Mantle, and John McGraw were summoned to bear witness, Subway Series 2000 was not a continuation of a storied tradition, but a parable about New York in the first year of the twenty-first century. This was a Subway Series for a city of newcomers and immigrants, yearning to write their chapter in the city's biography; a New Economy city oddly uneasy in a moment of global triumph. Sure, it was nice to watch the old film clips of yesterday's legends, but for most New Yorkers, those mythic images were from a long-gone and unknowable time—Civil War daguerreotypes in the age of the Gulf War.

Rather than luxuriate in past glories, the New York of Subway Series 2000 was determined to hang on to the momentous present, fearing the uncertain future. To achieve that end, to keep winning, to maintain their hegemony, New Yorkers will follow the rules of the new marketplace—they will outsource their champions if that's what it takes to remain competitive. This was the autumn of Hillary Clinton, late of Washington, Arkansas, and Illinois, brought in to represent a state she barely knows; the autumn of Roger Clemens, the ex–Red Sox, ex–Blue Jay mercenary whose behavior must be explained away as the price of continued victory.

Hillary Clinton and Roger Clemens were two of the many bargains New Yorkers made to keep moving away from the awful years of the late 1980s and early 1990s, when *Time* magazine famously ran a cover declaring the city dead and ungovernable. So it seemed. But soon the deal-making began. New Yorkers elected a mayor who promised a restoration of order; with the promise fulfilled, New Yorkers look out at a homogenized Times Square, read about rough and sometimes deadly treatment of innocents, and wonder. Prosperity came with order, but the newspapers soon noticed a revival of sweatshop labor. The homeless disappeared; few felt comfortable in asking where they might have gone.

In the same spirit of deal-making, New York Democrats, desperate to hold on to a Senate seat that has been theirs since 1976, signed up an outsider with a famous name and a record of fabulous fund-raising to keep their winning streak intact. Yankee fans found themselves demanding, then cheering for, the services of any available superstar, regardless of past history or excess baggage, to ward off the prospect of defeat. In mid-season, they yearned for Sammy Sosa and Juan Gonzalez, arguing with an odd sense of entitlement that great players ought be playing in New York. Damn the cost! We want to win! We're number one! We're New York!

This desperate gluttony betrayed a fear that Subway Series 2000 might, after all, have had something in common with the most recent Subway Series, in 1956. New York in the mid-fifties, we now know, was at the apogee of the old city of cherished memory, the New York of Robert F. Wagner and Herbert Lehman, of Mickey, Willie, and the Duke, of intact families and blue-collar white-ethnic neighborhoods. That New York vanished within a decade with the coming of highways that led to suburban housing tracts. By the mid-1970s, the city was on the verge of bankruptcy, and the neighborhood around Yankee Stadium was in flames. And an all–New York World Series seemed an irretrievable part of a long-gone golden age.

Subway Series 2000 was the climax of another and unexpected golden age, a milestone in New York's remarkable revival and in the narrative of the new New York, the city of Latinos and African Americans and Asian immigrants who weren't born when Don Larsen pitched his perfect game in 1956. New York in the 1990s had beaten crime, turned prophets into liars, welcomed tourists, and basked in celebratory television shows like *Seinfeld* and *Sex and the City*. But even as the millennial city celebrated its monopoly over the Fall Classic, the business pages chronicled the deaths of once-promising dot-coms, Wall Street and the Nasdaq continued their retreat from the giddy highs of a year ago, companies quickly pulled their initial public offerings, the country prepared for the end of the Clinton administration, and the city chatted about a post-Giuliani era. Faces that had become familiar during the great ride of the 1990s were about to become memories, and their places were to be taken by unknown or uncertain hands. Real estate agents accustomed to sixteen-hour days found themselves with time on their hands, their cell phones silent. Kids in Silicon Alley got the first layoff notices; they hadn't repealed the business cycle, after all.

So the cheers for Todd Zeile's bases-loaded double, which ensured the Mets of their fourth pennant, and for David Justice's three-run homer, which put the Yankees in the Series, were the cheers of an otherwise edgy city. Was this 1956, the end of something wonderful?

There was a poignancy to those cheers, too, for it was the sound of the new New Yorkers who knew all about the glories of the 1950s, who had been led to believe that they had missed something special. But now they had a Subway Series, a golden age, of their own. More to the point, this Subway Series featured names like Luis Sojo and Mariano Rivera; Timo Perez and Edgardo Alfonzo. The city of immigrants embraced these immigrant ballplayers as warmly as Brooklyn embraced the boys of summer who lived down the street, or just a subway ride away.

For today's boys of summer, however, there was little time for celebration. The Series was not in the record books a day when Yankee fans were demanding the services of high-priced free agents like Mike Mussina and Manny Ramirez. Met fans insisted that their club required the costly talents of free agent Alex Rodriguez. This was the only way to compete, to stay on top, to keep winning, they said. Old heroes would simply have to go, just as David Wells, who adored wearing Yankee pinstripes, had to be sacrificed to bring in Roger Clemens. The new economy has little patience for sentiment. Did some local Democrat yearn to be a U.S. senator? Too bad. Hillary Clinton, with her Illinois-Arkansas enthusiasm, was brought in to succeed Daniel Patrick Moynihan, of Hells Kitchen.

It's all about winning. It's all about the marketplace. It's all about New York in the twenty-first century. Make your deal, and explain later.

Terry Golway is the city editor of the *New York Observer*.

THE METS WIN!
THE METS WIN!

ANDY BOROWITZ

AS A DIE-HARD METS FANATIC, I'm disappointed that the team didn't accept Mayor Rudolph Giuliani's invitation to take part in Monday's ticker-tape parade down the Canyon of Heroes in lower Manhattan to honor the World Series champions.

Why? As any true Mets fan knows, the Mets actually won the Subway Series.

True, if all you're looking at are the final scores of the five World Series games, the Yankees were, technically speaking, the winners, but only in the narrowest sense of the word. To determine who really won the World Series, one has to look beyond the scores to the numbers that really count:

Which team was host to more Subway Series games at its stadium? The Yankees played host in the first two World Series games at Yankee Stadium, but the Mets, in a stunning comeback, held the last three

games at Shea Stadium. By this measure, the Mets edged the Yankees, 3–2.

Which team had more players named Franco? The Yankees failed to produce a single player named Franco in any of the five Subway Series games, while the Mets, in the clutch, came through with two key Francos, John and Matt. Mets win, 2–0.

Which team had its players' names on the backs of their jerseys? In this key contest, the "we're-too-cool-to-have-our-names-on-our-shirts" Yankees were no match for the clearly labeled National League squad. Mets win, 1–0.

Which team inspired more use of rhyming slogans? The "Let's/Mets" rhyme featured prominently in "Let's Go, Mets," while "Wave Your Hankies for the Yankees" never really caught on. Mets shut out the Yanks.

Which team had more players who did not throw a jagged piece of wood across the playing field? In this crucial category, the two teams were very evenly matched; still, the Mets edged the Yankees, 25–24.

Which team was the answer to the five questions above? The Mets win again and this time, most impressively, in a 5–0 sweep.

Now that I've established, once and for all, that the Mets won the Subway Series, the only remaining question is whether or not the Yankees will decide to show up at the parade. Personally, I hope they do. Otherwise, they run the risk of looking like sore losers.

———————

ANDY BOROWITZ is a writer and performer who contributes humor to *The New Yorker* and *The New York Times*. He is the author of *The Trillionaire Next Door* (2000).

———————

THE DIRTY DOZEN

ERIC BOGOSIAN

WAIT A MINUTE, WAIT A MINUTE, the Mets, pal, the Mets could never have won it. Never. Because you're talking about destiny. Heroism, larger-than-life shit. See? Because these Yankees, these are not *any* Yankees. Okay? These Yankees are larger-than-life human beings. Bigger than big. Historic. Mythic.

I figured it all out when I was up the other night goin' through my card collection. It was about three o'clock in the morning. And I had sorted out all the cards by year, team, league and division, you know? Committing stuff to memory, just in case, you know, Regis called and I had to know Donnie Mattingly's batting average in 1991, stuff like that there, you know?

And what should come on TV at that exact moment, but the greatest movie ever made, *The Dirty Dozen*, and then it all became clear to me why the Yanks were who they are. They are the dirty dozen:

they are a bunch of fatally flawed heroes given a chance for immortality, and they grab it by the balls.

See these Yanks, they're kinda misfits, see? And they need to win, they must win, for redemption. That's the way it works. Think about it. In the original movie, the team of commandos was made up of a bunch of guys who were like condemned criminals, right? Killers, nut jobs, manic-depressives.

And the Yanks, that's what they are. They all got some kinda checkered past. Take David Justice. Right? A little loose with his hands. Roger Clemens. Right? It's a miracle he hasn't killed anybody yet. These guys should be locked up. Instead, they're playing major league baseball.

Or they're not playing with a full deck a cards. Like Chuck Knoblauch. Right? He's not all there, but at the same time, he's awesome? Right. All guts. Wound a little too tight and very religious. Kind of the Telly Savalas of the group. And how 'bout Mariano Rivera. A cold-blooded assassin. Never talks, just like Charlie Bronson. Intense. Kills you with one lightning move of his arm.

How about Paul O'Neill? Troubled, guilty-looking, angry. He's the John Cassavetes character. Simmering, simmering, you never know when he's gonna blow. Or kooky, talented but kooky, Derek Jeter. Like Donald Sutherland. Big joker, all goofy and loose, laughing at the fastballs, cracking gum while he guns you down with the double play. It's all a big joke. Ha-ha. Here's another home run up yer ass.

And remember the big guy, the hillbilly, what's his name, Clint Walker? That's Jose Canseco. And a course, you got Tino, who would be the Trini Lopez guy, right? Brosius is Richard Jaeckel, dependable, heroic. Whoever's in left field is Jim Brown. Running, running, poppin' those hand grenades on top the Nazis' heads. *Boom! Boom! Boom!* They call 'em the Bronx Bombers, right? El Duque, a refugee; Conie with his fucked-up arms; Mike Stanton, maybe not the sharpest pencil in the box.

And you say, okay, Bernie Williams, what's fucked up about him? His eyes, you know? Had that laser surgery. How about that?

And see, the thing that makes all this work is Joe Torre. 'Cause he's Lee Marvin, the leader who doesn't take any shit from anybody. Been through it all. Tougher than the toughest. Knows his men. Takes 'em to hell and back. Never smiles. Never flinches.

And who's his trusty sidekick? Don Zimmer/ Ernest Borgnine. Eyes poppin' out, cheeks puffin'. Easily excitable. Really one of the boys, but also, you know, one of the officers, too.

And then the enemy is slightly crazy stick-up-the-ass Robert Ryan. Who else but Bobby Valentine! Right? Right? Really psycho, genuinely psycho because he's got a fatal flaw too. He thinks he's so smart no one can outsmart him. And that's how they beat him. With tactics.

And wait a minute, I'm not done. I'm not done. I've got proof! You know who directed the *The Dirty Dozen*? Robert Aldrich. Who's Robert Aldrich? His first picture was probably the greatest baseball movie ever made, *The Big Leaguer* for MGM back in 1953, which is the same year Joe Torre got called up from the minors. I think. I gotta look that one up. Fifteen years before they made the movie. See how it all connects? It all fits together.

That's why, pal. That's why. The Mets could *never* win. Never in a million years. 'Cause you're talkin' destiny. And you do not fuck with destiny, my friend. You do not fuck with destiny.

Bartender, two beers here.

ERIC BOGOSIAN is an actor and writer. His plays include *Talk Radio* and *subUrbia.* His first novel, *Mall,* was published in November 2000.

APPENDIX:

THE
SUBWAY SERIES
ANALYST

PETER HIRDT

THERE HAVE BEEN 564 World Series games. Of those, 182 were played in New York City (32 percent)—more than were played in the Central, Mountain, and Pacific time zones combined (166). The Yankees have hosted 100 (94 at Yankee Stadium, 6 at the Polo Grounds); the Giants, 41; the Dodgers, 28; and the Mets, 13. From 1947 through 1956, 49 of the 59 World Series games were played in New York (including 42 of 46 from 1949 through 1956). . . . Who played in the most Subway Series games? No, it's not a Yankee—though Yogi Berra and Phil Rizzuto are tied for second-most, just one game behind the leader. Pee Wee Reese played 44 World Series games for Brooklyn against the Yankees, the Subway Series high. . . . Some other Subway Series leaders: Duke Snider has the most home runs (10) and RBIs (24); Reese is the leader in hits (46). Frankie Frisch has the highest batting average (.375) and Dave Bancroft the lowest (.145) among players with at least 50 at-bats. Allie Reynolds leads all pitchers in wins (6).

◆ ◆ ◆ ◆

The Mets (94–68) and Yankees (87–74) had a combined regular-season winning percentage of .560, the fourth lowest by World Series opponents. The three Series with lower combined marks: 1973—A's vs. Mets (.545); 1997—Marlins vs. Indians (.551); and 1987—Twins vs. Cardinals (.556). . . . The Yankees' .540 percentage during the regular season was the second lowest by a Series winner, trailing only that of the 1987 Twins (85–77, .525). . . . Bobby Valentine made his World Series debut after winning 960 regular-season games. The only skipper with more regular-season wins before his first appearance managing in a World Series was Joe Torre (986 in 1996). And, like Torre, Valentine never appeared in a postseason game as a player. . . . Valentine played under Torre for parts of two seasons with the Mets. Three other managers faced World Series opponents for whom they had previously played: Rogers Hornsby (vs. Miller Huggins in 1926); Charlie Grimm (vs. Joe McCarthy in 1932); and Gabby Hartnett (vs. McCarthy in 1938). . . . Torre was an active player when hired to manage the Mets on May 31, 1977. He held the dual role of player-manager for less than three weeks. Torre's final game as an active player was on

June 17, which was also Bobby Valentine's first game with the Mets. (Valentine had been acquired from San Diego two days earlier in exchange for Dave Kingman—the same day the Mets traded Tom Seaver to Cincinnati.)

♦　♦　♦　♦

Ernie Banks, eat your heart out: Timo Perez debuted in the majors 50 days before starting in Game 1 of the 2000 World Series. Only five players started Series games in less time after their major league debuts: Buddy Myer, 1925 (14 days after debut); Joe Sewell, 1920 (25); Jack Sheehan, 1920 (29); Jimmy Moore, 1930 (38); and Jack Phillips, 1947 (44). . . . Benny Agbayani, Jay Payton, and Timo Perez, the Mets' starting outfielders in the first four games of the Subway Series, started only two games together during the regular season. In fact, they had played a total of only 379 regular-season games in the outfield. The only World Series team whose starting outfielders had less experience was the 1951 Giants. Monte Irvin, Willie Mays, and Hank Thompson, who started together in five games of the '51 Series, had a total of only 302 regular-season games of outfield experience. Clint Hartung, who started the other game of that Series in place of Thompson, had played only 11 more regular-season games in the outfield than Thompson had. . . . Jose Vizcaino was the tenth player to collect four hits in his

World Series debut. The last to do so were Paul Molitor and Robin Yount in Game 1 of the 1982 Series. (Molitor had five hits in that game.) . . . Al Leiter allowed more hits to left-handed batters in Game 1 of the Subway Series (3) than he had in any of his previous 36 regular-season starts, dating back to September 4, 1999. (For the record, Leiter also allowed three hits to left-handed batters in his previous start, Game 2 of the NLCS vs. St. Louis.) Paul O'Neill and Tino Martinez were the first left-handed teammates to get hits off Leiter in the same inning since Mark Grace and Mickey Morandini of the Cubs did so on August 1, 1999. . . . D.H. Fallout: Todd Pratt became the first catcher since Steve Yeager in 1981 to start Game 1 of a World Series after starting fewer than 40 regular-season games. Yeager started 23 games in 1981, his opportunities limited by a players' strike. Pratt made 38 starts behind the plate, and he hadn't started with Leiter on the mound since August 8, spanning Leiter's last nine regular-season starts and his first two in the postseason. During the season, Leiter's ERA was 2.87 with Piazza catching, 4.96 with Pratt behind the plate. . . . As a curiosity, Pratt became the fourth player to be hit by two pitches in a Series game. The others all happen to be Hall of Famers: Max Carey, 1925; Yogi Berra, 1953; and Frank Robinson, 1961. . . . Luis Polonia's single in Game 1 was his first hit in eleven career pinch-hit appearances in the World Series (10

ABs, 1 BB). He previously pinch-hit twice for Oakland (1988) and eight times for Atlanta (1995–1996). Polonia now holds the career record for most World Series games as a pinch-hitter (12), passing Johnny Blanchard and Vic Davalillo (10 each). The distinction of having the most Series pinch-ABs without a hit reverts to Dale Mitchell, who was 0-for-6. (His strikeout to end Don Larsen's perfect game was pinch-AB 5.)

♦ ♦ ♦ ♦

Roger Clemens had seven days of rest between his one-hitter in the ALCS (which he pitched on six days' rest) and his victory in Game 2 of the Subway Series (8 IP, 0 runs). During his career, Clemens has made 48 regular-season starts with six or more days of rest. (That includes his first start in each season, regardless of days after his last preseason start.) He is 27–7 in those games, with a 2.71 ERA. . . . With Clemens facing Mike Hampton, Game 2 was only the fourth in World Series history, and the first in more than fifty years, in which each opposing starting pitcher had thrown a shutout in his previous start. The other three: Christy Mathewson vs. Chief Bender in 1905; Howie Camnitz vs. Wild Bill Donovan in 1909; and Steve Gromek vs. Johnny Sain in 1948. . . . John Franco became the second-oldest pitcher to win a World Series game. Dolf Luque of the Giants beat the Senators to clinch the 1933 World Series in Game 5 at the age of 43. In Game 1, Franco became the twentieth player born in New York City to participate in a Subway Series. Five are Hall of Famers: Frankie Frisch, Lou Gehrig, Waite Hoyt, Phil Rizzuto, and Whitey Ford.

◆ ◆ ◆ ◆

El Duque, who won Game 2 of the 1998 World Series and Game 1 in 1999, failed in his attempt to win Series games in three straight seasons. Prior to 1960, and especially during the Yankees' mid-century dynasty, this wasn't rare; a total of fourteen pitchers have done it. But since Whitey Ford (1960–1962), only Catfish Hunter and Ken Holtzman have won games in three consecutive Series (1972–1974). . . . Yankees pitchers struck out at least ten batters in each of the first three games of the series. The last time they did that in three straight regular-season games was in May 1982—a bullpen-aided streak of games started by Ron Guidry (8 SO), Tommy John (3), and Rudy May (9). . . . Paul O'Neill had hits in five consecutive at-bats against left-handed pitchers over three games (Games 2 through 4). That equaled the longest such regular-season streak of his career, and it fell one short of the all-time World Series mark for left-handed batters, set by Lou Brock in 1968. Willie Stargell also had a 5-for-5 streak vs. southpaws, in 1979. . . . O'Neill became the tenth player to triple in consecutive World Series

games (Games 3 and 4); he had no triples in 566 at-bats during the regular season. . . . When Bernie Williams homered to lead off the second inning in Game 5, he snapped a streak of six consecutive World Series starts in the cleanup position without either a hit or an RBI. That is the longest such streak in Series history. He shares the mark with Red Murray, who was 0-for-21 for the New York Giants in the 1911 Series. . . . Derek Jeter became the first shortstop to hit home runs in consecutive World Series games. . . . Luis Sojo's Series-winning single snapped the Yankees' string of 15 hitless at-bats with runners in scoring position. It was the longest such streak in World Series play since 1997, when the Marlins had an 0-for-18 streak with RISP snapped by Edgar Renteria's Series-ending single. The Yankees' streak stretched back to the eighth inning of Game 2, when Tino Martinez increased their lead to 6–0 with an RBI single that provided the eventual margin of victory in a 6–5 win. . . . Al Leiter is 0–3 (with a 4.36 ERA) in eleven postseason starts, the most by any pitcher who has never won one. For the record, he has won a postseason game in relief—Game 1 of the 1993 World Series for the Blue Jays. In his seven post-season starts with the Mets, Leiter has left with a lead four times. (Armando Benitez blew saves in three of them.)

◆ ◆ ◆ ◆

Each of the last fifteen times a postseason series started with an extra-inning game, the team winning Game 1 won the series. The last team to win a postseason series after an extra-inning defeat in the first game was the 1958 Yankees in the World Series vs. Milwaukee. (The team that won Game 1 has won 11 of the last 13 World Series and 58 of 96 overall.). . . . During their NLCS victory over the Cardinals, Mets batters drew 27 walks while striking out only 24 times, becoming the first team since the 1992 Atlanta Braves with more walks than strikeouts in a League Championship Series. The Mets then became the first team with as many as 48 strikeouts and as few as 11 walks in a World Series. . . . The Mets' first- and second-place hitters posted a combined .217 on-base percentage, the lowest such mark by any World Series team since, oddly, the 1976 Reds. The Bicentennial edition of the Big Red Machine swept the Yankees, outscoring New York 22–8, despite sub-par performances by lead-off hitter Pete Rose (3-for-16) and second-place hitter Ken Griffey Sr. (1-for-17). . . . Yet in the 2000 Subway Series it was the Yankees whose leadoff hitters posted the lowest on-base percentage from that slot since the 1930 Cardinals. Yankees first-place hitters reached base safely only four times—two walks and two hits— in twenty-six plate appearances. The hits were Derek Jeter's home run on the first pitch of Game 4 and his triple on his next at-bat. . . . Jorge Posada started all sixteen postseason games for the Yankees in 2000—in

fact, he played every inning of every one of those games. In five seasons in the majors, Posada had never started more than fourteen straight games behind the plate, a high he reached during the second half of September 2000. His total of 158 games caught during the 2000 regular- and postseasons combined was two short of the all-time high, set by Randy Hundley of the Cubs in 1968 (all in the regular season). Darren Daulton also caught 158 games in a season, for the 1993 Phillies (146 regular-, 12 postseason). . . . Nine Yankees were on the team's roster in all four World Series appearances in five seasons under Joe Torre: David Cone, Derek Jeter, Tino Martinez, Jeff Nelson, Paul O'Neill, Andy Pettitte, Mariano Rivera, Luis Sojo, and Bernie Williams. It's often argued that free agency has increased player movement, enabling a team to "buy a championship." But that's the same number of players as the Yankees had on their World Series roster for all five years of their reign as world champions from 1949 to 1953: Hank Bauer, Yogi Berra, Eddie Lopat, Johnny Mize, Vic Raschi, Allie Reynolds, Phil Rizzuto, Charlie Silvera, and Gene Woodling. . . . Only three players won their fourth World Series at a younger age than Derek Jeter (26 years, 4 months): Joe DiMaggio (age 24 in 1939), Mickey Mantle (24 in 1956); and Billy Martin (25 in 1953). . . . At 28 years of age, Andy Pettitte became the youngest pitcher on the World Series roster of four championship teams. Three pitchers won their fourth title at age 29—all of them Hall of Famers: Lefty Gomez, Whitey Ford, and Sandy Koufax.

———————

PETER HIRDT is executive vice president of the Elias Sports Bureau and coauthor of *The Elias Baseball Analyst* series.

———————